Hindu Power in the 21st Century

Resistances, Fears and Obstacles

BY THE SAME AUTHOR

Arise Again, Ô India!

A Western Journalist on India: The Ferengi's Columns

A New History of India

A History of India as it Happened

In Defence of a Billion Hindus

Hindu Power in the 21st Century

Resistances, Fears and Obstacles

François Gautier

HAR-ANAND
PUBLICATIONS PVT LTD

HAR-ANAND PUBLICATIONS PVT LTD
E-49/3, Okhla Industrial Area, Phase-II, New Delhi-110020
Tel.: 41603490
E-mail: info@haranandbooks.com/haranand@rediffmail.com
Shop online at: www.haranandbooks.com

Published by Ashok Gosain and Ashish Gosain for
Har-Anand Publications Pvt Ltd

Printed in India at Vinayak Offset

Prologue

Why a book about Hindu Power, you may ask? Firstly, as I will explain at length all along, Hindu power is absolutely *secular* in essence, as Hindus have always accepted the diversity of the Divine: that He or She manifested at different times of our human history, using different Names and different Scriptures. Thus a Hindu will have no problem entering a church, a gurdwara, a mosque even. But the reverse, specially when it comes to Christians and Muslims—is not true. It has been thus a one way traffic for thousands of years and Hindus, on top of that, have been at the receiving end of Islamic violence and Christian missionaries to convert them—and this is the second reason why Hindus MUST take power—and keep it.

Thirdly, I am one of the very-very few western journalists and writers to defend Hindus (some people speak of Mark Tully—but after having covered Kashmir with him in the 90's, I can tell you that he is not such a staunch defender of Hindus). I was a born and brought-up as a catholic and knew absolutely nothing about India, Hinduism and Hindus. When I was a young Frenchman of 19, I had the privilege to hear about the Mother and Sri Aurobindo, through a friend, whose father was the last Governor of Pondichery. My friend told me that a caravan of 5 cars was about to drive from Paris to Pondichery. On a hunch, I joined this caravan.

Upon arriving in Delhi after driving trough nine countries, I felt I had come home and that this country was a very special place.

I lived in the Pondichery Sri Aurobindo ashram for eight years. These were wonderful times: the Mother was still alive and everything looked new, everything seemed possible. One read Sri Aurobindo, of course, as he was the Master and the inspiration of the place, but one either did not understand or felt disconnected to his political writings.

Then, having done some journalism and photography in France, I started freelancing in South India and I discovered the Hindus. What I chanced upon was that their religion was not in their heads, as it is for us Christians—"I must pray, I must be good, I must not sin"—but that it was rather something they lived: they seemed, for instance, to accept me, a Westerner, a non Hindu, as they seemed to accept all other religions. This discovery would never leave me, even when I became a political journalist in Delhi for major French newspapers.

Thus slowly, I became acquainted with the eternal principles of Hinduism:

- A Hindu is one who searches for the Ultimate Truth.
- Unlike other religions, Hinduism refuses to sanction the monopoly of one God, or one Scripture as the only way to salvation.
- Hinduism is the eternal faith, Sanataana Dharma, or the universal law by which all humans are governed.
- Hindus believe that the soul takes birth in a physical body, dies, gets reborn, until it has attained Perfect Divinity.
- Hindus consider that one can cleanse oneself from karmas through yoga practices, such as pranayama, meditation or asanas.
- One can be a Christian, a Muslim, a Jew, or from any other religion and still practice Hinduism. His Holiness Sri Sri Ravi Shankar has shown the way: breath has no religion and pranayama can be practiced by anybody, whatever their creed.

In that sense, I could consider myself a Hindu—at any rate I decided to stand-up for them, as they have been killed, hounded, persecuted, made fun of, derided—and it's still happening today.

Contents

CHAPTER 1

The Awakening

As a young journalist, I was prone to all the clichés that abounded then – and are still there (though much less since Mr Modi came to power)—about India: 'Congress is the best 'secular' party to deal with India's diversity; the British brought democracy: railways, a universal language and education; Hindus can also be 'fundamentalists', etc,—but Mother India opened my eyes. In the early eighties, when I started freelancing in the South, doing photo features on Kalaripayat, the Ayappa festival, or the Ayanars, I slowly realized, *on the ground*, that the genius of this country lies in its Hindu ethos, or rather in the true spirituality behind Hinduism. The average Hindu that you meet in a million villages, possesses this simple, innate spirituality in his or her genes and accepts your diversity, whether you are Christian, Muslim, or Jain, Arab, French or Chinese. It is this 'Hindu-ness' (which cannot be experienced if you sit in Delhi most of the time) that used to make most Indian Christians different (unfortunately today Indian Christian missionaries have imposed on converted Christians a purdah-mole religion), from say a French Christian, or an Indian Muslim unlike a Saudi Muslim. I also learnt that Hindus had given refuge to all persecuted minorities of the world, whether the Syrian Christians, the Parsis, the Jews (India is the only country in the world where Jews were not persecuted), the Armenians, or today the Tibetans. In 3500 years of known existence, Hindus have also never military invaded another country, never tried to impose their religion upon others, by force or even by induced conversions.

Thus for me, you cannot find *less* fundamentalist than a Hindu in this world and it saddens me when I see that the Indian and Western

Press always try to equate terrorists, such as ISIS, who blow up innocent civilians, to angry ordinary Hindus who only express their ire on Social Media. We know that most of communal incidents in India, such a the ones that happened in Orissa a few years ago, often involve persons of the same caste, Dalits and tribals, some of them converted to Christianity and others not. Furthermore, as I will show later, however reprehensible was the destruction of the Babri Masjid, no Muslim was killed in the process; compare this with the 'vengeance' bombings of 1993 in Mumbai, which wiped-out hundreds of innocent, mostly Hindus. Yet, the Babri Masjid destruction is often described by journalists as the most horrible act of the two. We also all remember how Sharad Pawar, when he was CM of Maharashtra in 1993, lied about a bomb that was supposed to have gone off in a Mumbai Muslim locality.

I have never been politically correct, but have always written—not what is the prevalent trend—but what I have discovered while reporting . Let me then say that Hindus, since the first Arab invasions, have been at the receiving end of terrorism, whether it was by Teimur, who killed 100,000 Hindus in one day in 1399, or by the Portuguese Inquisition which crucified Brahmins in Goa. Today they are still being targeted: there were one million Hindus in the valley of Kashmir in 1900—but only a few hundred today, the rest having been made to flee through terror. Hindus, the overwhelming majority community of this country, are being made fun of, are despised, are deprived of the most basic facilities for one of their most sacred pilgrimages in Armanath, when their Government heavily sponsors the Haj; they are witnessing their brothers and sisters converted to Christianity by financials traps, reading of blasphemy about their Gods…

Today there are about a billion Hindus, one in every six persons of this planet, one of the most successful, law abiding and integrated communities in the world. Can you call them terrorists?

CHAPTER 2

The (Past) Story of Hindu Power

Once upon a time Hindus had power: emperors like Chandragupta, who was advised by the remarkable Chanakya (also known as Kautilya), possessed territories so vast, that they extended from Karnataka till the present day Afghanistan. His soldiers were feared by enemies—in fact, contrary to what western history books tell us, Alexander the Great, who had the most powerful army of this time, encountered tremendous resistance in India and had to retreat, dying from his wounds on the way back to Greece. Yet, Hindu power had discrimination: battles were only fought between *kshatriyas*, during the daytime and the crops and lives of farmers were *never* touched. Hindu power could also be 'soft': contrary to Christianity and Islam, Hindus never sought to impose militarily their religion and way of life to other nations. Yet, Hinduism went peacefully towards the East and can still be seen today in Bali, Laos or Cambodia, witness Angkor Vat; and towards the West, where it had a great influence on the Greek and Celt philosophy and religion.

The administration that Chanakya and Chandragupta established, was so remarkable that it was later used by the Mughals and the British with little modifications. Many more great Hindu civilisations then rose-up: in the South, for instance, the Pallavas of king Simhavishnu conquered Ceylon, as well as annexing the Chera, Cholas and Pandya kingdoms. We owe them the superb sculpted temples of Mahabalipuram and powerful cities such as Kanchpuram. Under their rule, Sanskrit went through a revival period and the mandapam technique of temples flowered like never before, as did the Bhakti movement, which gave a fresh dynamism to Hinduism. In the

Centre of India, the Vardhamana dynasty of king Harsha, added Bengal and Orissa, to an already powerful empire that included today's UP, Bihar, and even spread northwards towards Nepal and Kashmir. French historian Alain Danielou wrote « that King Harsha symbolised all that was right in Hindu monarchy, wielding an absolute power, but each sphere of administration was enjoying a large autonomy and the villages were functioning like small republics ».

Even after successive centuries of violent Arabs invasions, Portuguese and Chinese travellers still marvelled at the land of 'milk and honey' that India was, where practically 'no beggars could be seen'. The last great Hindu Empire was that of Vijayanagar, where the kings also ruled in a *dharmic* manner and provided justice, education to all, freedom of religion and the flowering of art and culture. Historians tell us that the sacking of Vijayanagar was one of the most bloody ever in the history of India: rivers ran red with bloods for days, ten of thousands of Hindus were brutally killed, the looting went for six months, all the statues had their noses and ears chopped and every Muslim soldier went back to his land with a bounty of gold, horses, women and slaves....

Hindu power then vanished *for nearly 450 years*. The British, who rightly understood that Hindus were the principle obstacle to their colonising the land and the minds of India, further undermined Hindu Power by dividing India on the lines of religion and castes, a legacy that lingers even after Independence, as well as shaping-up in Cambridge and Oxford an elite class of Indians whose descendants today still think and act British. In 1947, Nehru who had already embraced the British idea of socialism, saw to it that Hindus still be denied any form of power, by promoting other religions, erasing from history books most traces of Hindu greatness, taking over Hindu temples, and restraining the few Indian Hindu nationalists, whom he had to admit to his Govt, such as the no-nonsense Sardar Patel.

In the year 2000, Hindus at last came back to power, when Atal Bihari Vajpayee was elected Prime Minister of India. Hindus had great hope in him, but Vajpayee, in true Hindu tradition, showed lack of insight, by giving orders to leave Sonia Gandhi alone and driving to Lahore in a 'peace bus', while Pakistani President Musharraf was sending his disguised soldiers to take over the Kargil hills. The BJP was also complacent, thinking that the little bit economic progress they brought to India, would be enough to win the next elections. But he Congress was re-elected for ten years and Mrs Gandhi, far from being grateful, mercilessly went all out after the BJP and Narendra Modi. And once more, Hindu power was snatched away.

Then Narendra Modi appeared on the All-India scene: he was a remarkable chief Minister of Gujarat, making of his state the most prosperous in India, the less corrupt, the greenest and the only one where ministers actually worked for the people— instead of for themselves or their parties. Many did not forgive him for not calling the army immediately after the anti-Muslim riots, triggered by the burning of Hindu pilgrims in the Sabarmati train, but that did not stop him from positioning himself as a prime ministerial candidate and he was cleared of any wrongdoing by the courts.

More than even Vajpayee, Mr Modi became Prime Minister of India in 2014 on a *united Hindu vote*, from the Dalits to the Brahmins. Hindus voted Narendra Modi to power, because he pledged many things that they had been yearning for a long time: a Common Civil Code, the removal of article 370, or the building of the Ram temple in Ayodhya. They also liked the fact that Modi was a fiery Hindu, so different from Vajpayee: he called a spade a spade, was not afraid of naming his enemies and was a passionate and eloquent orator. Modi thus became Prime Minister of India with a huge majority, and all Hindus hoped that power had come back to them after 5 centuries, for at least several generations.

Modi, did an outstanding job in his first mandate: he initiated economic reforms, such as pushing through the much needed GST bill, inaugurated a Clean India movement which is indispensable, given the present state, restored some of India's international reputation by making a number of visits abroad and tried to streamline the bloated Indian bureaucracy. Some who voted for him, were a little uneasy, because they did not recognize the outspoken, no-

nonsense Gujarat CM, in Modi the Prime Minister of India. They understand that as the leader of all Indians, Modi had to rise above partisanship, but they also realized that there was not really during his first mandate a true re-establishing of Hindu power, as temples continued to be under government rule, Indians still could not buy land or open businesses in Kashmir, while Muslim Kashmiris were selling everywhere in India their carpets and shawls, and the Chinese continued to bully India, even blocking its access to the nuclear club (NSG). The reelection of Modi in 2019 and his coming good on many of the pledges he had made in the campaigning of 2014, such as the removal of Article 370 in Kashmir, reassured many Hindus and bides well for future Hindu power, as it looks like the Congress' decline is for good.

Why then are there sill a few Hindus who feel that Mr Modi may have lost touch with what they expected—rightly so, as they elected him? It is true that Delhi is a big bubble, plonked all the way up in the North, far from the South, even the Center of India where everything is decided, often in an a arbitrary manner, where journalists, politicians, diplomats, huddle together in seminars, parties and embassy cocktails, repeating the same clichés, which in turn are taken-up by foreign correspondents: secularism, 'Hindu fundamentalism' or the eternal obsession of all Indologists—for India's caste problems (whereas since Independence, if there is one thing that the Indian Congress did, it is to work on promoting lower castes, and that quite successfully). Furthermore, while in Gujarat Modi, was in the right in the Center of India, and made himself available to contacts, meeting many people from all walks of life, in Delhi, he is surrounded by a quadruple layer of security, innumerable PA's, PS's, high bureaucrats, ministers, which is all a Congress legacy, a straightjacket that he, nor his ministers are trapped into, even if it is against their will. But Modi proved them wrong by showing, thanks to Amit Shah, his Home Minister and architect of the 2019 election victory, that he was not afraid to tackle the issue of Kashmir and the unjust and arbitrary Article 370, which evoked international criticism when he removed it.

In the next years, that are remaining with him, the Prime Minister needs thus to *please* his Hindu electorate, in the same way the Congress has shown that it always pleases its own traditional Muslim and Christian voters. There has to be some more hard decisions, that are mid-way to those he pledged before being elected, such as removing Govt control on Hindu temples, introducing a common civil code, or clamping down on the growing Islamic fundamentalism in Kerala or West Bengal. Mrs Sonia Gandhi had for ten years an Advisory Board, and in this way she was able to get some feel about what the people of India desired. Why did Modi refuse the same proposal that was put up in front of him, so that every month he listens to the opinions of a rotating board of twelve representatives of Indians from business, religious, societal, or cultural spheres? These would be one way that he gets opinions different to those he receives from his own cabinet, high bureaucrats and entourage who often give "yes ministers" opinions in true Bhakti tradition. Modi, while keeping a certain imperial aloofness, needs too to show a *tougher* image than the one he is projecting now—versus the Chinese for instance that are still claiming huge chunks of Indian territory, built a road between Sinkiang and Pakistan, and are surrounding India from all sides, from Nepal to Burma, from Sri Lanka to Pakistan. Hindus need to be protected: India is the only country in the world where Indians have become refugees in their own country—remember the 400,000 Hindus of the Valley of Kashmir, who where chased out of their ancestral lands and houses by violence. Hindus are also persecuted in Pakistan, Bangladesh, or even Fiji and need support. As one tweeter said: "we need a Putin of India not a second Vajpayee."

Hindu power however will always be compassionate: : Hindu are the inheritors of the last Knowledge that can save the world: what happens after you die, what is karma, what is dharma, what is an avatar and how the soul which is God's spark in you, reincarnates itself from life to life. Narendra Modi was elected to protect this Knowledge and he cannot fail this task. In today's world, it is necessary, to have not only economic, but also military and even nuclear power, otherwise, as China showed, a nation doesn't earn any respect. And today India is not respected the way it should, considering that contrary to China, she remains a vibrant democracy. Modi thus needs to flex his muscles, while retaining the qualities of all Hindus which is compassion and love.

Finally a quote from the avatar of the 20th century, Sri Aurobindo: "Unhappy is the man or the nation which, when the divine moment arrives, is found sleeping or unprepared to use it.... But thrice woe to them who are strong and ready, yet waste the force or misuse the moment; for them is irreparable loss or a great destruction."

CHAPTER 3

The Prithviraj Chauhan Syndrome

It is worthwhile here to recount the story of Prithviraj Chauhan and Muhammad Ghori, because it has a strong moral for today.

Prithviraj Chauhan was born at Ajmer in 1166 A.D. and Muhammad Ghori in 1149 in Afghanistan. Ghori's obsession was India, which he attacked savagely many times, though he was first routed in present day Gujarat by Rajputs and again in Kayadara near Mount Abu, in 1178 A.D. He then decided to enter India through the Khyber pass and first encountered Prithviraj Chauhan at the battle of Tarain in 1191. Prithviraj's cavalry charged, overpowered the Muslim cavalry and captured Ghori. Ghori begged for his life and Prithviraj allowed him to go, despite his generals telling him not to do so.

And surely enough, the following year Ghori came again. Prithviraj advanced with his army and sent a letter to Ghori, asking him to turn back as he had been already defeated was spared his life. Ghori replied that he was in India on the orders of his brother, Ghiasuddin, and that he could only retreat after he got a word from him. This letter was sent in the evening and thereafter Ghori moved his camp back a few kilometres to feign retreat. On receiving this letter and seeing Muhammad move his camp back, Prithviraj assumed that Ghori got the message. But Ghori, knowing that Rajputs did not fight in the night, attacked in the early morning hours when Prithviraj and his army were sleeping and thus was able to win this one battle. 40,000 Rajputs were taken prisoners and executed and 22,000 women and children were captured and enslaved.

Prithiviraj was beaten-up and taken in chains to Ghor in Afghanistan There, he was presented before Ghori and fearlessly looked straight into his eyes. Ghori who ordered him to lower his eyes, whereupon Prithiviraj told him how he had treated well Ghori as a prisoner and that the eyelids of a Rajputs are only lowered in death. On hearing this, Ghori flew into a rage and ordered that Prithviraj's eyes be burnt with red-hot iron rods.

Prithiviraj was regularly brought to the court to be taunted by Ghori and his courtiers—and ultimately put to death.

Narendra Modi has been re-elected PM. Will he, again, like a good Hindu, like Prithviraj Chauhan, forgive Sonia and Rahul Gandhi, who have been mercilessly going after him when the Congress was in power for ten years, ruthlessly and shamelessly using the arms of the law, the CBI, the IB, the judiciary, compliant judges, the Election Commission, etc.?

Don't laugh: as we said earlier, Vajpayee did it before him. He was elected PM and could have done anything he wanted, but gave orders to leave Sonia Gandhi alone. His Friday man, Brajesh Mishra, is even said to have rescued Rahul Gandhi, when he was caught in the US with a suitcase full of dollars. Did it earn Sonia Gandhi's gratitude? Not at all! The BJP lost the next elections, as Prithrivaj lost his next battle to Ghauri, and Mrs Gandhi mercilessly went all out after the BJP and Narendra Modi. If she could have had Modi imprisoned, or maybe indirectly killed by Islamic terrorists, as nearly happened when her Home Minister, Chidambaram, knowingly let terrorist Ishrat Jahan in to Gujurat, where she and her companion were plotting to assassinate Narendra Modi when he was the CM.

It is thus important that Narendra Modi goes after the Gandhi family now that the BJP is again in power. There are plenty of legal justifications to do so: the Gandhi family have stolen from India huge amounts of money: in the Forbes list, Sonia Gandhi is listed one of the richest politicians in the world. Priyanka's husband has unethically multiplied his fortune by 600 times in a few years. Moreover, this family who has ruined India since independence, and it has ruthlessly been after Hindus, side-lining them, ostracising them, imprisoning their gurus, allowing Islamists to bomb their temples and kill them.

Modi's second task is to decentralize the government away from

Delhi. He should build an entire new capital away from Delhi, which remains a Congress bastion, in Indore, Ujain or Pune, for instance, so as to break the bureaucratic hold that is still hanging around India's neck and the VVIP culture, which is synonymous with Delhi .For he BJP's last tenure has proved three things: (1) That the Indian (and foreign press) do not really reflect the people's sentiments; (2) That at some point the BJP lost sight of the Indian voters' sentiments. (3) That the BJP tried to please the Indian press and foreign media (and failed).

May God protect Modi and the mistake of Prithivaj Chauhan be not repeated.

CHAPTER 4

Vijayanagar, a Battle Twice Lost

It was once called the "Royal Avenue", running from the great Virupaksha temple complex, to the majestic Nandi at the bottom of Matanga Hill. An avenue of exquisite and mighty proportions, where, during King Krishna Devaraya's reign, such pomp and festivities happened, that Portuguese traveller Domingo Paes, said that "Vijayanagar is the best provided city in the world."

But today, the royal avenue presents a sad sight to the many western tourists: ramshackle shacks, dubbing themselves "restorents" have been erected all along, in clear violation of the UNESCO rule (which granted Hampi the status of World Heritage); trash is lying everywhere alongside with brackish water, breeding millions of mosquitoes; every second man is a beggar and you are constantly hassled by children asking you for pens, touts and hordes of postcard sellers. Welcome to Hampi the most beautiful and priceless archaeological site of India!

And if only the money thus earned by the Archeological Survey (which, for 70 years, was busy covering up the fact that most mosques in India, including the erstwhile Babri Masjid, were built on ancient Hindu temples) is used to better the place. But their idea of improvement seems to put strands of barbed wire here and there (no tree planting) and propping up a few temples with stones walls (whereas they could use India's craftsmen to reproduce some of the pillars in ancient style). Many of the exquisite temples are unattended, their statues half broken or lying on the ground. Indeed, the Japanese, who had given crores of rupees for the upliftment of Hampi have withdrawn in disgust and the Unesco has threatened to do the same, unless the very ugly bridge being built on the Anegondi side is stopped (it has been, for the moment) and illegal construction near the sites halted (it has not).

Yet, the Hampi ruins are without doubt the most extensive, the most beautiful, the best-preserved pieces of Hindu Power in India. Very few here know that Vijayanagar, the greatest Hindu empire ever, was, in the words of French historian Alain Daniélou, "like an island of civilization, chivalry, and beauty, in the midst of a shattered and bleeding India after nearly seven centuries of Muslim invasions." Numerous travelers, from Italian Nicolo di Conti, to Persian Abdul Razzak or the Portuguese Fernando Nuniz, have marveled at Vijayanagar's incredible richness, its incredible refinement, or the amazing water canals devised by its kings, which still work today and make of the Hampi region one of the most prosperous rice belts of India. Nearly five centuries later, you stumble in the middle of nowhere upon an extraordinary Ganesh sculpted in the rock, or a reclining Vishnu abandoned in a lonely temple. What a stupendous civilization and culture, which poured so much love and devotion on hard rock, whose mottos of beauty and respect to Gods and Nature, can still be witnessed today, in spite of the murderous hand of the Muslim invaders.

For when Ramaraya was betrayed (by the Lingayats?) on January the 26th 1565 (today nothing had changed: Hindus still betray Hindus) and his head cut, it was a holocaust: "during nearly five months, writes Danielou, the soldiers of Husain Nizam Shah set themselves to the task of destroying everything and the scenes of terror and massacre were unparalleled and mightier than the imagination can ever fathom. The victors grabbed so much richness, that there was not a single plain soldier who did not depart a rich man and the most beautiful and prosperous city of that time lay in smoking ruins." Today, at every corner of Hampi, you can witness the mark of the Muslim's deep hatred for anything Hindu: most of the noses, breasts, arms, legs, elephants trumps of the statues, have been broken by the soldiers of Nizam Shah, as well as the houses and the royal palace; and it is only because the temples had been built in such a solid (definitely quake-proof) fashion, that they have survived till today for our own wonderment.

Yet one finds that Indians themselves seem to have little regard for this extraordinary inheritance. The guides talk loud, know little and are just interested in fleecing the westerners; and the local people, even though many of them are making a good living out of these very ruins, show no respect for their own patrimony: Hampi is a vast excremental dump: there is dung from the thousands of bony, famished looking cows and goats everywhere; and as there are no public toilets, people are relieving themselves near and even inside the temples, or on the rocks leading to the ghats; and even the Indian tourists coming by noisy busloads, seem to have little empathy for these wonders.

Europeans are taught right from school to revere Greek and Roman culture and a pilgrimage to Athens or the Coliseum is a must for everybody. As long as Indian children will not be told of the greatness of Vijayanagar and taught that the Muslim holocaust which took place there has been negated, we cannot expect an improvement of the situation. As for the Indian Government, it should relocate all the non-farmers elsewhere, make the whole Vijayanagara area a national park and allow shops and restaurants only on the outer boundaries. Only then will the wonder that is "the City of Victory", be preserved for future generations and Hindu Power be rekindled in the 21st century.

CHAPTER 5

Hindu Power (The Downside)

I have been praising and defending Hindus so much in the last thirty years, through my articles, books and conferences, that I may be allowed to criticize them too: **Hindus are the worst enemies of Hindus and of a rebirth of Hindu Power**. There is no way that foreigners could have invaded India without Hindus having betrayed each other, from Alexander the Great, who allied himself with the Hindu king of Taxila (Ambhi) against Porus, also a Hindu, to the sack of Vijaynagar, the last great Hindu empire, which was betrayed by the Lingayats. Today, Hindus still undercut Hindus—the community of exiled Kashmiri Pandits is so divided that you hardly ever hear heir voices; Hindu associations in the USA vie with each other for a photo opp with a Congressman, instead of coming under one united umbrella, to have the kind of lobbying power that the Jewish community for instance possesses; even the RSS, which is called the HSS there, often snubs other Hindu organizations. The most lethal enemies of Hindus in modern India are Hindu intellectuals, whom you find in every newspaper, every think tank, every American or British university, always ready to brilliantly denigrate their own culture. I have defended the BJP from the beginning, when MM Joshi went to plant the Indian flag in Srinagar, which I found rather patriotic, (Narendra Modi was also present) though the entire Media made fun of him; and when LK Advani did his Rath Yatra. But I soon discovered that Advani and Joshi could not stand each other and that Vajpayee made sure that Advani never became PM. Today we saw Arvind Kejriwal, a Hindu, always question Narendra Modi, another Hindu.

I have criticized Islam so much in the last thirty years, through my articles, books and conferences, that I may be allowed to praise them here. There is a universal brotherhood amongst Islam: when I drove from Paris to Delhi, in a caravan of five cars, my best friend was a French Moroccan Muslim, named Ahmed Mzali (he has unfortunately died since then). In every Muslim country, we crossed—Turkey, Iran, Afghanistan, Pakistan—he would say 'Salaam Alaikum', and people would smile, open their doors, feed us, shelter us... Try to say 'Om Namah Shiva' to a Hindu in New York, London or Delhi: either he or she will look nonplussed, or most likely give you a dirty look! Indeed, Muslims all over the world are proud of their religion and flash it without any self-doubt. But look at Hindus: many of them are ashamed to be Hindus, to the point that sometimes they wallow in self-denial. Islam has established some moral boundaries which attract new converts to them: no alcohol or smoking for instance. Whereas alcohol is a huge problem in Hindu India, from the villagers who spend their salaries on cheap arrack, beat up their wives and spoil their health, to rich kids who think it's hep to down a bottle of Black and White whisky in one evening.

We know now that Muslims will die for their beliefs – in fact they will go on murderous sprees if they think their God has been insulted, even as a joke – see what happened in the Charlie Hebdo murders in Paris, an attack that has been silently endorsed by millions of Muslims in the world. But look at Hindus, you can insult their Gods and Goddesses as much as you want – and nothing will happen to you. The painter M.F. Husain knew that very well and that's why he painted Goddess Laxmi, naked, or Sita being sodomized by Hanuman. He should have asked himself what would have happened to him if he had been a Hindu insulting Islamic beliefs in such a crude and disrespectful manner! Though Muslim countries have their own agenda, they stand by each other – and this is why Pakistan gets so much support in the UN. Every Muslim in the world feels for Palestine, Chechnya or Kashmir. But a billion Hindus in India and worldwide did not give a damn about 400,000 of their own becoming refugees in their own country, for no other fault than being Hindus. If you are a Muslim, you are likely get help anywhere in the world. But Hindus must be the most selfish and individualistic people on this planet. They rarely care about their brothers and sisters in need and those of lower castes. This is why a Mother Teresa is able to come here and do the work that Hindus should have performed themselves, thereby bring to India the worst image possible, that of a country that leaves its old people die on the pavements and abandons children.

Most Muslims pray 5 times a day, wherever they are in the world. I would say that maybe 6% of Hindus in the United States or the UK perform pujas or go to temples regularly. The rest have thrown their religion in the dustbin. It's not a question of religiosity, but of using tools and checks that you help your life move in a meaningful and straight direction. As there is no concept of sin in Hinduism, but only of karma, Hindus must be amongst the biggest tax cheaters in the world, they mix ashes in cement, methanol in alcohol for drinking, and have no respect for their environment, littering their country with millions of plastic bags polluting their rivers, and devastating their forests. All our Muslim friends, rich or poor, make sure that their children learn the Koran at a young age – but Hindu kids have no clue about their great scriptures, the Bhagavad Gita, Ramayana or Mahabharata. Thus modern Hindu adolescents grow into adults with no respect for their temples and deities. Muslims have reverence for their ancient language, Urdu (formerly Persian), whereas Sanskrit, probably the most scientific language in the world, has fallen in disuse and no Hindu kids want to learn it. Muslims still worship their historical heroes – even Aurangzeb for instance, revered in Pakistan (and in most Indian and western history books), through he was a murderer, not only towards Hindus, but with his own family (he beheaded his brother, poisoned his father Shah Jahan and imprisoned his son). Hindus have no clue about their heroes and heroines: Shivaji Maharaj, India's Napoleon, is described as a small chieftain and plunderer in most history books; as for Maharana Pratap, the only Rajput who actually fought the Moghols and held Akbar at bay, he is only known in northern India and he too is undercut in history books. Muslims have finally a sense of community and tend to live together in towns and villages, so as to preserve their identities and customs. Hindus in contrast, want to merge wherever they live, in the US for instance, and often become more American than the Americans, thereby forgetting all about their roots.

Thus Narendra Modi has a huge task in front of him if he wants to truly rekindle a sense of brotherhood and civic senses amongst Hindus, that would in turn generate true and dharmic Hindu Power. Therefore the need of the hour for Hindus is: UNITE, UNITE, UNITE and the first sign of this collective will, would be a Hindu united vote, from the Dalit to the Brahmin, that will carry again the BJP to power in 2024, so that Modi may finish his work and break the Hindu jinx of betrayal and fear.

CHAPTER 6

Hindu Power and Resistance to Change

One expected resistance to Narendra Modi's reforms – economic, social and judicial – from the Christian and Muslim communities, as well as the Marxists. No surprise here: same as during the time of the Vajpayee Govt, Christians have been busy at portraying themselves victims of "Hindu fanaticism", so as to get India a bad image abroad, even though Modi went out of his way to make them feel safe. The removal of Kashmir's article 370 has added to India's bad image in the West, fuelled by the Social Media, a sure sign that the Muslim community in India is not that cooperative. Again we see that the Prime Minister made a lot of efforts to woo the Muslims, receiving the likes of Bollywood Amir Khan, who had signed petitions against him when he was Gujarat CM, meeting mollahs, etc. But many of us know that 95% of Indian Muslims will never vote for the BJP in next elections. Indeed, we always point the finger at Pakistan, but let me tell you, for having covered Kashmir extensively, that it is the Kashmiri Muslims *themselves*, from the retired High Court judge, to the Shikara boatman, who want to separate from Hindu India, and that in the name of Islam. They are the ones moaning at the moment, because at last Modi has bifurcated Kashmir into two union territories. Pakistan is only using this discontent for its own selfish purpose, mostly because it wants revenge for the breakup of East Pakistan into Bangladesh, for which it holds India responsible. The same is true of the November 2008 Mumbai attacks: nobody ever bothered to find out who were the local Muslim scouts and suppliers of information, as it's too embarrassing for a Hindu majority Government to admit that it is its own Muslim community which may want and trigger such attacks – witness the thousands who attended in Mumbai the burial of Yakub Memon after he was hanged.

But nobody expected resistance from the Hindus themselves, who stand to benefit most from a Hindu majority Govt, for which they voted in overwhelming majority in 2014and 2019, from the Brahmin to the Dalit. This resistance takes three forms. It's firstly that cheating and corruption has become so ingrained in Hindus' DNA, that it will take a long time to erase them. We believed that the Prime Minister's demonization, Aadhar move and drive for transparency, would effect a change. But we see around that Hindus continue cheating without blinking and any sense of guilt at all – I am not talking here about Christian guilt, but about a sentiment, as dim as it may be, that they are harming their country's wellbeing. It was all right to cheat when the socialist policies of Indira Gandhi taxed the so-called rich 90% – but today, Indians are not taxed anymore than in any democratic European country.

The second form of resistance is cleanliness. There may be some pockets where the Swaach Bharat is working – for a show to the PM, but I tell you, as I travel extensively throughout India, the country has even become *dirtier* since Modi started his movement. Just go to the Old Delhi station and see the huge garbage on the track and people throwing without a second thought all kind of empty packages through the windows of their compartments. As the train starts its journey through UP, everywhere it's an endless sight of plastic, garbage, mud and dirt. You think Delhi is better? You should see Lodhi Garden on Sundays by 6PM: it is littered with thrash and nobody even gives it a thought. It's as if people go at it with a vengeance.

The third resistance of Hindus is indiscipline. Nothing symbolizes it more than the way Indians drive. I recently crossed Uttrakhand from Delhi – it's crazy: people overtake you from the right or the left, on the highway innumerable cars drive confidently on the wrong side, coming at you with blazing headlights. If there is a jam, everybody will try to cheat by inching forward, creating even more confusion. This too is cheating and is deep-seated in Hindus. I also went to Haridwar with my mother in law's ashes. I saw coke bottles floating in the Ganges, plastic bags, trash. On the banks, not only Pandits keep asking for money and loot shamelessly the family of the dead, repeating mechanically mantras without any heart, but also I noticed that some of their lackeys dive in the water, to retrieve the gold or the coins the dear ones have thrown. Nobody here can blame the Muslims or Christians – and it plays in the hands of Marxists who say that Hinduism is a devious religion – so sad. The Dalit community too, is falling prey to this indiscipline: it is being used again by the Congress and is being split, so that a chunk votes for the Congress. It's unfortunate and they should read again their guru, Ambedkar, who was a true nationalist and did not mince his words.

People will say that all this cheating, tamas, indiscipline, is karma or fate, or indifference. But those who are in the spiritual life, know that there are occult forces behind the scenes that move men and make them do things without them being conscious of it. These asuric powers are against evolution, against change, and they are very active at the moment, particularly against Mr Modi and his endeavour to change India. Anybody who has tried to transform himself or herself, will have experienced this inherent unwillingness to transformation in human nature, this resistance to the Divine.

Finally is Modi himself unconsciously resisting Hindu Power? That's a good question. Nobody can doubt his sincerity and his drive, working 18 hours a day and keeping on initiating new projects to improve the life of Indians and inject more dynamism in its economy and foreign affairs. But in Delhi, a huge bubble, far away from the rest of India, he seemed to have softened and lost the ear he had on the ground when he was CM of Gujarat. Many of his Hindu hard-core supporters who voted him to power, are disappointed, as he has not implemented all of the pledges he made, the Ram temple, or a common Civil Code etc. Also he seems to be a victim of the bureaucracy, both the high one, who keeps advising him to be prudent and moderate, as well as the middle one and lower one, who resist his changes, as their power will diminish.

And this raises the question: are Hindus, the most ancient people ever in the world, going to miss on the great Renaissance Narendra Modi is trying to bring, because of their resistance to change? Are they going to put in jeopardy the survival of the last great Knowledge that can save the world – because of their tamas?

The solution would be that Modi will realize at some point that he is a prisoner of a system created by the Congress – the VVIP culture, that the BJP seems to have adopted so smoothly, the corruption in politics, and the immense power the bureaucrats have on India – and that he will try to break from all these shackles and bypass the bureaucracy to go directly to the people. We wish to see again the fiery no nonsense Modi, who, in the true spirit of the Bhagavad Gita, will become the fearless warrior who fights – ruthlessly if needed – not only against India's external enemies, the Chinese and the Pakistanis, but against the internal enemies, those Hindus at all levels – the poor who litter, the rich who cheat, the high bureaucracy, which always advises restraint, and the lower corrupt bureaucracy which clings to its petty and corrupt power.

CHAPTER 7

Hindu Power, 2nd Part: Corruption and Black Money

After Narendra Modi's brilliant stroke against Black Money and Corruption, which go hand in hand, it's worthwhile to ask this question: are Hindus more corrupt than others? We will look only at Hindus and l leave aside Muslims, as they were the masters of India for so long, and in their heydays, As Aurangzeb proved, they need not be corrupt – only pitiless against Hindus. The same is true of the British, who made their riches out of India and did not have to cheat their own Government – and hence the class of Anglo-Indians they had fashioned to be the go between them and the 'natives' was not that corrupt either. India's 3% present Christian minority is thus excluded from this study. We will be also be looking at statistics and facts over the last ten centuries, as it will give a more complete overall picture.

As I said earlier, I have defended Hindus enough – lately through series of articles and this book on Hindu Power. That I may allowed to criticize them: Hindus of today – and yesterday – are indeed corrupt, deal a great deal in black money, cheat their Government, whether it is Congress or others, from the attendant at the petrol station to the richest CEO in Mumbai. But let me beforehand excuse them.

First of all, Hindus have been so heavily traumatized by ten centuries of savage Islamic invasions, that cheating, breaking the line, finding the loophole, hiding, became a matter of sheer survival. Hindus were killed, their women and girls taken as slaves, their temples razed, they were forbidden to ride horses or palanquins, and more than anything, they had to pay a heavy and humiliating tax , the jyzia... Naturally cheating and hoarding happened – and it became a habit – even after it was not needed anymore.

Secondly, at Independence, Nehru, who was a great admirer of the British socialist system, chose to tax the rich for empowering the poor. Industries and individuals were levied up to 90% of their revenues for decades and of course they cheated. Once more it was more the Hindus, as Muslims were often in the less fortunate categories and Christians a tiny minority. It can also be added that the poor, under successive Congress Governments, never really benefited from whatever amounts the taxmen got from the rich, as bureaucrats took their cut on the way down.

Thirdly, as explained above, contrary to Christianity, there is no concept of guilt in Hinduism. Thus, there is no moral brake to corruption and black money, as there is in the West, and I have often observed that Hindus from the poor to the rich, do not feel they are doing something wrong when they are defrauding their own Government. I will never forget in Almora seeing a village woman cutting a young tree sapling for firewood, in an already dwindling forest, and when we pointed it out to her, she said: "so what, it belongs to the Sarkar"....

The paradox is that in my 40 years in India, I have come across so many honest Hindu Collectors, police officers, bureaucrats and I have *never* been asked for a bribe, maybe because of my white skin. Yet living in Delhi, I know for a fact that my foreign correspondents fellows pay extravagant prices for renting their flats in Jorbagh, Golf Links or Defence Colony – at least 40% of which are in cash or on foreign accounts, most of them owned by Hindus. I remember how horrified a colleague from LeMonde newspaper was, when she asked the owner of a Sujan Singh Park flat in Delhi (a part shareholder of the Imperial, New Delhi), were was the bathroom for the servants – and he told her nonchalantly that they could go to the public toilets of Khan Market! This dreadful attitude can even be seen at airports today, where there are no toilets for the staff, even in Delhi's Terminal 3, and they crowd the passengers' toilets. I know also that builders in

India are the most corrupt and the ones who hoard the maximum black money. Anybody knows that to buy a flat, you need to pay 40% in cash. Again, most of these contractors are Hindus.

Hindu politicians would have suffered too from the demonitazion. How will they buy the one laptop per student, or the one TV per household, that they dispense by millions like lollipops, at the time of elections? How will all the Mulayam Singhs, Stalins, Mayawatis, Mamta Banerjees, deal with this huge cash problem? How will the Hindu leaders of the Congress – yes, 97% of Congressmen and women are Hindus – get the cash to buy votes, or MP's, as shown by the cash for votes scam, exposed by Suddhendra Kulkarni? We thought that we would indeed see a great transformation in Hindu politics, thanks to the 500 and 1000 Rs notes ban – but it seems the politicians found a way to go around it, as there is no lessening of corruption in politics. We see today in the recent election in Haryana that it's a small party the JJP, of Dushyant Chautala which held the key for some time of who was going to be the next Chief Minister. In my journalistic career I have witnessed this scenario so many times: they will extract their pound of flesh not only in terms of minister's berths, but also in hard cash. This is democracy hijacked.

In conclusion, it is the *system that triggers the temptation to corruption*. Hindus, because of tremendous colonial and invasional traumas, have made of cheating a habit. Nehru prolonged it, by severely taxing the rich and not so rich. Now Mr. Modi has opened a channel to reverse this trend. It is first in *their minds*, that Hindus must lose the habit of cheating. Then will it happen on the ground.

A true Hindu power has to be honest, Chanakya and so many others great Hindu kings, the last one being Krishna Deva Raja of the mighty empire of Vijaynagar, have shown that true Hindu power is *Dharmic* in spirit, that is honest, hardworking and generous to all, irrespective of their ethnic origin or religion. One must congratulate the BJP Government for having initiated what in 40 years of power since Independence, the Congress did not dare to do.

CHAPTER 8

Another Obstacle to Hindu Power: Are Hindu Cowards?

« Hindus are cowards and Muslims bullies », the Mahatma Gandhi once famously said. And this seems to be fairly true: today at the least sign of trouble, Hindus stay home, shy from confrontation, or outright run away. We indeed witnessed how the 400,000 Hindus of Kashmir, who had done no crime, except being Hindus, fled the Valley of Kashmir under terror, without firing a single shot in self-defence, losing all their ancestral homes and lands and becoming refugees in their *own* country. Hindus who are also persecuted in Bangladesh or Pakistan, and even in West Bengal, in districts where illegal Bangladeshis outnumber them, rarely defend themselves (except under the lone and courageous Tapan Ghosh). In Assam, where the same situation arises, it is the Christian Bodos who took up arms, not the Hindus. How is that possible, when Hindus are still nearly 80% of India and have their own government, that of the BJP, in power at the Centre?

Many have tried to analyse this weakening of the Hindu psyche, that resulted in a loss of power for 450 years. Among the causes that have been spoken off, we find Buddhism's uncompromising stance on non-violence, which seems to have blunted the Kshatriyas spirit of the Hindus. But that cannot be the total explanation, as Buddhism was wiped out of from India by the successive Muslim invasions, whereas Hinduism survived. Various historians have also pointed out that the biggest genocide in the history of Humanity must be that of the Hindus: from the time of the Hindu Kush (which means the killing of Hindus), when Muhammad Ghori, after having defeated *Prithviraj* Chauhan, took away in winter 50,000 slaves to Afghanistan, the majority of whom died of cold in the Kyber pass, to Timur, who killed one hundred thousand Hindus *in one day*! it has been calculated that *100 millions Hindus* died, directly or indirectly, because of invasions. This has left a scar of terror in the Hindu collective unconscious, that can be observed even today, as we said earlier.

Certainly, the British colonisation, though it was much less brutal, left a mark in the Hindu consciousness: Hindus learnt not to think for themselves but to reason the way the British did. From great innovators, they became brilliant copiers. The English also fashioned an Indian intellectual class, surviving till today, which looks at India through British eyes, that is negatively, often with contempt and misunderstanding. Mahatma Gandhi added his bit, by his refusal to see the harm that was done to India by his always accommodating Jinnah's demands, and his equally rigid insistence on non-violence. Indeed, though most history books credit the Mahatma with the freedom of India, it is early revolutionaries, such as Sri Aurobindo or Gangadhar Tilak (see later chapter), who believed in the re-igniting of Hindu power and the booting out the British, by force if necessary, who where its true initiators. Guilty too, the first Prime Minister of India, Nehru, who thought that his country did not need a powerful army, which led to the disastrous defeat against the Chinese in 1962. He also compromised on Kashmir, when the Indian soldiers had the upper hand, and went instead to the UN, thus, legating the problem that is flaring up today in the Valley. It is this combination of Buddhism, Gandhism, colonisation, Nehruvianism and trauma of invasions, which have eroded, not only Hindu power, *but also the capability of Hindus to hold power and wield it efficiently* when they have it.

Therefore, Hindus, even when they come to head the government of India, have the tendency to stretch their hand first to the enemy, witness Vajpayee going in the 'Peace bus' to Lahore, while Musharraf was sending his soldiers to grab Kargil; or Narendra Modi attending Nawaz Sharif's granddaughter's wedding and then be caught of guard in Kashmir a few years back. **Compassion can only be exercised when you are strong and ready.** Yet, it is not that there is no precedent to learn from: a thousand years ago, as we have seen earlier, Mohamed Ghori rewarded Prithivaj Chahan's generosity in letting him go free, when he lost the first battle of Tarain, by attacking Chauhan treacherously a year later, blinding him and ultimately executing him...

The irony is that Hindus could take example on how to exercise power from one their most famous Scriptures, the Bhagavad Gita and the Kurukshetra war. There we see Krishna, telling Arjuna that on one hand in battle you only kill the body of your enemy – not the soul – as it is indestructible and is reborn later in another body; and on the other, commanding Arjuna to fight physically and ruthlessly, even against people whom Arjuna knows and loves, so that righteousness is re-established. This is what Hindus have lost today: the courage to fight for what they believe in, physically, if need be, and to be merciless against the enemy. The modern Kurukshetra battle today has to be fought against Pakistan, a nuclear nation that is manufacturing terror as others export cars; and even more with China, an intelligent, ruthless and deadly enemy, which is using Pakistan in its proxy war with India.

As we are talking about Hindu Power, we need here to stop and redefine the word 'Hindu', which is the subject of much misunderstanding. If one reads properly the Vedas, the Upanishads or the Bhagavad Gita, at no time is it mentioned that Hinduism is a religion. In fact, the word 'Hindu' never comes-up for centuries and it seems that it is first the Portuguese who used it to designate people who lived on the banks of the Indus river. Hindus believe in Dharma, the path of righteousness; but again nothing in common with the American notion of Good and Bad: what helps an individual or a nation towards self fulfilment is Dharma; and what impedes them, is a – Dharma – Chanakya had got it right. Hindus also believe that the soul takes birth in a physical body, dies, gets reborn, until it has attained Perfection. Finally, Hindus over the ages have fashioned tools to help them in their karma and dharma: pranayama, meditation asanas and all kinds of yoga – of devotion (bhakti), or knowledge (Jana), or perfection in work (karma yoga)....

In the old times, Indian Christians and Muslims were more integrated in this way of thinking: one remembers that Sufism was prevalent in Kashmir till the arrival of Pakistani and Afghan hard Sunni influence in the early eighties; or that Syrian Christians, till the coming of the Portuguese, had borrowed many Hindu local customs. Today even, an Abdul Kalam showed us that one could be a true Muslim, and still quote from the Bhagavad Gita; or Leander Paes, born Christian, demonstrates too, that all Christians can be proud to represent India and be great friends of Hindus.

Hence the taking over India by a genuine Hindu Power need not be feared by minorities and should be welcomed by the western and eastern world. For it would mean an India powerful, friendly, but when necessary ruthless, as was the case after the Balakot attacks. It will also, in true Hindu spirit, recognize and respect the wonderful diversity – religious ethnic and cultural – of this great and ancient country that is India...

Chapter 9

The Great (Hindu) Brain Drain

Did you know that the greatest brain drain in the world is – and has been – that of Hindus?

What started as a migration of coolies or indented labour from India towards Mauritius, Fiji or Madagascar, turned into the Great Brain Drain from the 60's onwards. Scientist, engineers, doctors, most of them Hindus, all looking for better salaries or opportunities, started immigrating to the US, UK, Canada and others countries, when it was still easy to obtain visas and eventually citizenships. In turn, in the 70's till now, Indian students applied for scholarships from great American and British universities – and often got them – as Indians are good students, capable of memorizing pages and pages of study materials (see how they always win the Spell Bees competitions). It therefore became a fashion to study in foreign universities for children of upper class and even middle class families.

Today, though India is doing much better economically, this trend is still going on and the best (Hindu) brains of India are still deserting their country. Did you know that 75% of British doctors are of Indian origin – and that the whole system would collapse if they would leave? 60% of the engineers of the famous Silicon Valley are Indians, and in the last 10 years, the migration of Indian engineers and scientists to the United States has increased by a whopping 85%!

In 2019-2024, under Narendra Modi's rule, when you meet any official in Delhi, bureaucrats or politicians, even from the BJP or RSS, and you ask where are their children, the answer will often be:

"Harvard, or Cambridge, or even McGill University in Canada." The sad thing is that these children and their children and their grand-children will never come back to India and are a loss not only to India, but even to the US or the UK, as they quickly lose their Indian-ness and bring nothing novel to their country of adoption.

They often do not have even gratitude towards India, who gave them education, most of the time free, and become more Americans than the Americans, more British than the English, sometimes even ashamed to be Indians. This Great (Hindu) Brain Drain MUST BE stopped. Indians, who have succeeded abroad, MUST be coaxed back to their native country and contribute to its present development, economical, political and even cultural.

How to do it? Well first, there is the negative indirect consequence of this tightening of visas in the US and elsewhere, because of the refugees' problem. This is unfortunate but the consequences can be seen as positive, as it lessens the Brain Drain. Good too the fact that westerners, Americans, particularly, are sometimes not able to differentiate between Arab refugees and harmless Indians. It will help Hindus in the US to start thinking about immigrating back to India, even if it is out of fear.

On the positive side, Modi should facilitate the coming back of NRI's. What he has done so far: the OCI, tax rebates, liberalising the economy, is good, but not enough. Indian Scientists in the NASA, for instance, researchers in American universities, teachers, doctors, which India needs so badly, should be offered more incentives to come back home: on par salaries and perks, affordable homes, and other facilities.

What the Chinese have also shown is that nationalism and the PRIDE to be Chinese, is the biggest incentive to come back. Thus, in the same way, the Indian Government should induce a feeling of duty and nationalism in NRI's: "Come back to your own country, help to make it a great nation, India is the future super power of Asia – of the world even..."

As a westerner, when I see those long queues in Delhi in front of the American embassy, I find that it is demeaning to this great nation that is India. And I dream that one day westerners will also queue to apply for working visas in front of Indian High Commissions into their own countries, because India – with the help of true Hindu power – will have become a land of opportunities. Thus the Great (Hindu) Brain Drain will be not only stopped, but also reversed.

CHAPTER 10

Hindu Power Needs an India that Innovates Again

Nowadays, Narendra Modi's mantra to entrepreneurs, or for that matter for the whole of India, is simple: « INNOVATE»... This is easier said than done. India used to be a country of *Innovation*, which gave to the world the zero concept, chess, Vedic mathematics, astronomy, philosophy... In fact, French astronomers up to the 18th century, used to say that ancient Indians knew before everybody how to calculate the distance between the earth and the moon. More than that, the influence of Vedantic philosophy on Greek thought and mythology, or of Vedic maths on the making of the Egypt pyramids, has been remarked upon by many Indologists, France's Alain Danielou being one of them. Even after the savage onslaught of Arab invasions, from the 10th century onwards, Chinese and Portuguese writers still marvelled in the 16th century at India being a land of 'gold and honey', where the 'iron never rusted', as symbolized by the Vishnu pillar, which is today in Delhi's Qtub Minar.

It is probably the British colonization that blunted for good the Indian innovation spirit. First, the English broke the backbone of rural India which had lived on barter for centuries – farmers would exchange part of their crops for whatever they needed from potters, weavers, food merchants etc, – by imposing crops they needed for their industrial revolution, such as tobacco or cotton, which led to widespread famines in the 19th and early 20th century (20 million Indians, 7% of the population of that time, died of famine in a 100 years, according to British statistics) ...And then the infamous

Macaulay decided that the only way to win India's heart, would be to fashion a class of Indians, educated in Oxford or Cambridge, that would think like the British and act as intermediaries with the 'natives'. This masterstroke heralded the end of Innovation in India, as Indian leaders started copying everything that the British did. At Independence indeed, Nehru, who was a great admirer of English socialism, adopted whatever the British had left – the constitutional, judicial, education systems, without caring to adapt them to the Indian psyche, which is unique and very different from the English.

The result today is that Indians lag three decades behind nations like China, which was in the same bracket as India at Independence, with overpopulation, an alphabetism and poverty. Take the manufacturing sector, for instance, since Independence, India has often copied English models, such as the Ambassador car, the Royal Enfield Bullet, or the Raleigh cycle, selling them at huge profits for decades and never caring much to improve them. Today we see even companies like Hero, who for decades produced the same heavy cycle and still do, partner with the Japanese to produce better quality products, then dump them unceremoniously after copying the Japanese models – and still not able to come up with anything really new. We also observe that since the much-hyped software revolution happened in India 20 years ago, Indian companies are still not manufacturing any hardware worth the name for computers, even more, no computers of international quality. Look in comparison at China's Lenovo, who has become market leader in the world! Indians have also not yet built their own plane, except for the Tejas, which is 23 years in the making and a white elephant. Compare this with the Brazilians, again a country very similar to India, in term of challenges, who have produced the Embraer, one of the best short haul planes in the world. This is not to say that Indians did not innovate at all – but when it happened it was the exception to the rule – like the Tatas for instance.

A word about Indian architecture, which used to be one of the most innovative in the world – witness Mohenja Daro, whose planning, houses, sewer systems, water supplies, were so good that it would take Europe quite a few centuries to catch-up. Today India is a vast jungle of concrete, city after city, town after small town in styles that were used in the 50's in the West and since then have been razed. See Gurgaon, an entire new city, where everything could have been built right! But what a mess it has been made off: hardly any trees have been planted, no proper drainage system, no uniformity of architectural style. It's only the five star hotels that have borrowed some of India's architectural genius and used indigenous materials, tiles, wooden pillars, inner courtyards, thatch ... Modern Indian art too, is a copy, brilliant or not, of western art and most of the time does not use any Indian-ness in its expression, Raza being one of the lone exceptions. And of course the ever-present Bollywood, often copies entire western films, not only the scripts, but scene by scene, dialogue by dialogue. Its actors never go to acting schools, do not sing, and their dances are speeded-up digitally so that they look slick.

Today Indian universities basically teach the same curriculum that is imparted in the West. As a result, what they produce are brilliant (Hindu) *clones*, who have no root in their own culture and are only good for export. This is in fact what happens: as most Hindus who go abroad, either as students, or on employment, eventually settle there and their children and grandchildren, are lost for India, without bringing anything of an Indian-ness to the United States, UK or Canada, which badly need it, as family values are lost there: 98% parents die now in old people's homes, three out of five couple divorce and people are stressed and often depressed. Thus it is clear that India does NOT innovate anymore.

What to do so that Indians become innovators again and not copiers anymore?

Firstly teach them about their own history: their poets, their warriors, their philosophers, their heroes and heroines. Again, let me say that as a Frenchman, I was brought up to be proud of Voltaire, Napoleon, Victor Hugo, or Charlemagne. India has amongst the greatest heroes, poets, writers, warriors in the world. If France had one Jeanne d'Arc, India has dozens of them: Rani of Jhansi, Ahiliabai, Chennama, Rani Abbakka, Rani Rudramma, Rani Velu Nachiyar, etc.

The British have Shakespeare, but India's Kalidasa, even translated from the Sanskrit, is one of the greatest poets ever, on par with Homer. But is he taught in schools? No! In warfare, we the French have Napoleon, but Maharashtra Shivaji Maharaj (see later chapter) should be a hero for Modern India: alone with a few hundred men, he stood against the most powerful army in the world of his time, with only his wits and extraordinary courage. He was also *secular* in nature, in spite of being an ardent Hindu: he never harmed the wives and daughters of his enemies did not touch mosques and donated to Sufi saints. He administered justly wherever he conquered, was incorrupt and built the first Indian navy. Yet, even in Indian History books, he is treated little better than a chieftain and is totally unknown abroad, whereas Napoleon is known in India. In Tamil Nadu, if you say Shivaji Maharaj, people think you are talking about the actor!

Indian students learn about Descartes or Kant, but India has Sri Aurobindo (see later chapter) who was not only one of the early revolutionaries, as 30 years before the Mahatma Gandhi, in the true spirit off the Bhagavad Gita, he thought that the British should be fought, not only a yogi, but also is one of India's most comprehensive philosophers. His 'Foundations of Indian Culture' or 'Synthesis of Yoga', are amongst the best ever on Indian philosophy and Thought. But is he part of the philosophical curriculum in India? Not at all. Nietzsche or Hegel, who were inspired by the Vedantic thought, are though!

As I will keep repeating all along this book, Hindus are the last holders of a Knowledge that has survived the millenniums: "what happens when I die; what is rebirth? How God manifests Himself or Herself at different times, using different names and scriptures; what is karma, what is dharma..." Today monotheistic religions think there is only one life, then heaven, purgatory and hell; or that if you blow yourself up in the midst of innocent people, you will go to heaven and enjoy 27 virgins, simplistic and superstitious beliefs. There are also ancient tools that have been devised by sages which are secular in nature, and can help modern Indians, whatever their religion and ethnic origin: Hindus should start using more Ayurveda (or Siddha or

Unnani), the most ancient medical system in the world still in practice, that knew long before western medicine that many illnesses have a psychosomatic origin and that plants and minerals are the best medicines; they should learn pranayama, the ancient science of breathing that gives me a more intuitive mind and a better energy; they should do more of hata-yoga, to give their body more suppleness and endurance; they should practice too simple techniques of meditation to de-stress themself; and finally: they should adopt, as the ancient Vedic sages the whole world as their family 'Vasudhaiva Kutumbakam', a unique concept that can save the world from the self-destruction path that it has embarked upon at the moment. The irony is that all these techniques, born in India, are now taking the West by storm, where most Hollywood stars fluently practice yoga, where pranayama is used for stressed executives' workshops and hata-yoga is being introduced in American schools, while India has turned its back to them.

What will happen when Hindus and Indians as a whole will adopt these techniques ? First a feeling of nationalism: "I am proud to be a Hindu" – not like often now: "am ashamed to be a Hindu" (see later chapter), as my intellectuals and Media keep harping about our poverty, castes wars, or fundamentalism; let me thus blend in the US and become totally American, or totally British." Secondly, "I excel in business, in arts, in entertainment, in sports, not only for myself, but also for my nation." And finally: "it's been a privilege to be born in a country where such an ancient Knowledge still exists, whereas it has disappeared from other ancient civilizations such as Greece, Egypt, or Mesopotamia; let me give me then back to my country a little bit." To paraphrase what Kennedy famously said for the US: "ask not what India can do for you, but ask yourself what you can do for India." Then will India INNOVATE again and excel at all levels.

CHAPTER 11

True Hindu Heroes and Heroines: Shivaji Maharaj

Who is just, firm and stands for the weak?
Who is an honest and able administrator?
Who confronts the enemy and is not cowed into submission?
To whom did Mother India appear in a vision to fight for victory?
Who has the statesmanship and the vision to build a Greater India?
Who is ruthless with his enemies, but spares women, children and his own people?
Who respects all religions and pays homage to Muslim, Jain or Hindu saints?
To which political party belongs this Hero for Modern India?

Actually to none. But Chhatrapati Shivaji Maharaj does belong to India and to *all* Indians, whatever their religion or ethnic origin, for he is an eternal icon of courage, statesmanship, love for his country, able and honest administration. In fact, the qualities that he embodied, are those that a modern Indian politician *should* possess, but unfortunately, seldom has. Shivaji was a man for all India: he travelled, thought about, and warred in all parts of India, from Agra, then capital of the Mughal empire to Gingee, all the way down in the South. He was the first one who understood that India needed a navy if it wanted to control its waters – and he did build a formidable one.

Yet, try to look for a biography of Shivaji in any bookshop in India: it is practically impossible to find one, as many have gone out of print. Most of these biographies, except, the one from James Lane, which has all the hostile flaws of western, date back to twenty to thirty years. Now, in my country, France, we have such a hero in Napoleon. All children are schooled into Napoleon's great deeds right from kinder garden. Like Shivaji, Napoleon was not only a great warrior, but also a statesman of exceptional vision: some of the laws and codes he devised, are still in practice today. Thus, most French people are proud of Napoleon – and rightly so – because he was, like Shivaji, great warrior, a visionary and an exceptional statesman. Therefore, every year, at least four to five new books are written, directly or indirectly, about Napoleon, his life or his deeds.

Compare this with India, where not only it is difficult to find a book about Shivaji, but where a few years ago, the Kerala Government put a ban on school notebooks which carried pictures of Chhatrapati Shivaji Maharaj... This is wrong. No nation can move forward unless it has heroes. No country can progress unless it is proud of itself and can make its children relate to heroes seeped in one's culture. But it is not so in India. This is not jingoism, but nationalism. Yet every time you open an Indian newspaper or switch on a TV channel, the impression you get is that everything is rotten in India, nothing works and that Indians are the most corrupt and inefficient people in the world.

Why is that so? Maybe because of three hundred years of British colonization, many of India's politicians, bureaucrats and journalists are often copying whatever the West does, or are eternally worrying about what the West thinks of them. They rarely think Indian, know all about Shakespeare, but very little of Kalidasa, one of the greatest poets ever on this Planet; have read about Abraham Lincoln, but know nothing of Sri Aurobindo, philosopher, poet, revolutionary, immense yogi. Many of India's intelligentsia have thus no idea about India's great culture, philosophy and spirituality. Very few have read the Bhagavad Gita, or understood that it encourages yoga in action and that sometimes it is important to defend one's country, culture and borders, by force if necessary, as Shivaji Maharaj practiced it.

There is also the wrong notion that Shivaji was anti-Muslim because he fought Aurangzeb. But the truth should be known: Shivaji allowed his subjects freedom of religion and opposed forced conversion. The first thing Shivaji did after a conquest was to promulgate protection of mosques and Muslim tombs. One-third of his army was Muslim, as were many of his commanders: his most trusted general in all his campaigns was Haider Ali Kohari; Darya Sarang was chief of armoury; Ibrahim Khan and Daulat Khan were prominent in the navy; and Siddi Ibrahim was chief of artillery.

Aurangzeb was a cruel man, even to his own family, as we already said: he killed his two brothers, threw his son in jail and had his father Shah Jahan imprisoned and later poisoned. Shivaji was the only one who stood up against him, at a time when Hindus were experiencing great oppression and humiliation: their temples were being broken, and they were being discriminated against in various forms, such as in the matter of charging custom duties, restrictions on their fairs and festivals, their dismissal from government posts, large-scale conversions as a part of openly declared policy of the Mughal State, imposition of the religious tax *Jiziya* for being a Hindu, and these discriminatory acts were going almost unchallenged though the Hindus formed more than bout 80 per cent of the population of the country.

Yet, Shivaji had respect for the Sufi tradition of Islam and used to pray at the mausoleum of the great Sufi Muslim saint Baba Sharifuddin. He also visited the abode of another great Sufi saint, Shaikh Yacub of the Konkan, to seek his blessings. He called Hazrat Baba of Ratnagiri *bahut thorwale bhau*, meaning "great elder brother". Shivaji's feelings are reflected in a letter he wrote to Aurangzeb: "Verily, Islam and Hinduism are terms of contrast. They are used by the true Divine Painter for blending the colours and filling in the outlines. If it is a mosque, the call to prayer is chanted in remembrance of him. If it is a temple, the bells are rung in yearning for him alone." Shivaji also applied a humane and liberal policy to the women of his state, irrespective of their religion, nationality, or creed.

What to do then to remind all Hindus of the great champion they had in Shivaji? I for one, am proud to say that our History Museum in Pune has TWO permanent exhibitions on Shivaji Maharaj, a champion of true Hindu Power. This is a small contribution of a foreigner, who loves India and think it is a wonderful country with great Hindu heroes and heroines.

Wake-up of my Hindu brothers and sisters. You are a great nation, you have great heroes and Shivaji, certainly, is one of the most endearing ones: a *Vibhuti*, a direct incarnation of God, who walked upon this sacred soil of India, fearless and yet humane; a Giant of a Man, who could be reached by all. He was truly A Hindu Hero for Modern India.

Chapter 12

True Hindu Heroes and Heroines: Ahilyabai Holkar

When prince Malhar Rao Holkar, ruler of the Indore state died in 1765 at the age of 76 years, he left behind him huge territories which yielded an annual income of seventy lakhs of rupees a huge sum for those days. His only son Khande Rao had died during the siege of Kumbher, a Jat fortress, a few years before, in 1754, leaving behind is own son, Mali Rao, which he had with his wife, the illustrious Ahilyabai. After Malhar's death, Mali Rao to cover his grandfather's extensive possessions, but died after a short reign of nine months. After his demise, the Government of Indore was conducted by Ahilyabai with the approval of Peshwa Madhav Rao, the Prime Minister, and the support of the Maratha Confederates.

From 1766 till her death in 1795, Ahilyabai ruled Malwa with such ability that her thirty year long rule is regarded as "model of benevolent and effective government." She had been trained in the State-craft as well as in the art of war by Malhar Rao himself. She had led Holkar's troops in person with four bows and quivers of arrows fitted to the corners of the howda of her elephant. After assuming power, she appointed Tukoji Holkar, one of her clan but not related to her, to the supreme command of her large army. In his appointment, as in all others, Ahilyabai showed an extraordinary sense of judgment, so much so that she kept "almost to the man, the same set of ministers and administrators throughout her reign."

Born in 1725, Ahilyabai had not the advantage of royal birth. Her father was the Patil (chief of a village), in Chondi Bhind district "Her entrance on the stage of history was something of an accident," writes Eleanor Zelliot, an American historian. She recounts that Malhar Rao was on his way to Pune when he stopped at Chondi for a while and saw the 8 years old Ahilyabai at the temple service in the Village. He at once recognized signs of piety, intelligence and nobility in the girl and brought her as a bride for his only son Khande Rao.

Ahliyabai never observed purdah (segregation of women in households) and held daily public audience and was accessible to the commonest of her subjects. Sir John Malcolm, one of a British officials of the 18th Century, writes about her, forty years after her death, "Her first principle of Government appears to have been moderate assessment and an almost sacred respect for the native rights of Village officers and proprietors of land. She heard every complaint in person and although she continually referred cases to the Courts of equity and arbitration ... she was always accessible, patient and unwearied in the investigation of most insignificant cases when appeals were made to her for decision."

In that period of instability and turbulence, Ahilyabai had "one of the most stable reigns of the 18th Century" so much so that her territories in Malwa were never "attacked or disrupted by local battles during her reign inspite of wars all around." All through her reign, her relations with the foreign princes remained most amicable and cordial. The comfort, happiness and peace enjoyed by his subjects, in whose prosperity she felt a peculiar solace and sense of fulfillment, during her 30 years of rule were unprecedented in the annals of Malwa. The accounts of the State were kept with scrupulous exactness under her care and no decision was taken by any of her ministers, and even by Tukoji Holkar, without her knowledge and advice, such as employment of a French Officer named Chevalier Dudrenee who trained four battalions of her army, or policy to act in concert with Mahadji Sindhia in resisting the march of English troops in Gujarat in 1780. The envoys residing at the courts of Indian potentates were all appointed by her.

During her 30 years of rule of Malwa, Ahilyabai received "that allegiance and respect from feudatories and sovereigns, which might well excite the envy of any prince or princess in any part of the country." Though an extremely pious lady, who devoted much of her time in offering prayers and in meditation, she was always ready to attend to any task which required her tact and skill. "She always evinced a maternal regard for the welfare of her subjects and under her they were so happy and contented that no Indian Sovereign in any age could boast of a more contented ryot." In fact, she rejoiced when she saw her people – bankers, merchants, farmers – rise to affluence, without ever the slightest tinge of cupidity.

Among her many accomplishments was the development of Indore from a small village to a prosperous and extensive city, though her own capital was nearby Maheshwar on the banks of Narmada river, from where she not only conducted the administration but also provided ample patronage to arts and letters.

She also built several forts and roads and "the deep ascent of the Vindhya Mountains was rendered passable by a road of easy slope, constructed at an enormous cost." Her works of charity and public usefulness can be the pride of any sovereign. She patronized and encouraged festivals, gave endowments for maintenance and regular worship in the temples and built a large number of temples, not only in Malwa, but outside also and embellished them, stretching from Badrinath in the Himalayas to Rameshwaram in the South. Among these are Kashi Vishvanath Temple at Varanasi and temples at Ayodhya, Mathura, Hardwar, Kanchi, Avanti, Dwarka, Jagannathpuri, Gaya etc.

Under her maternal care the state prospered and the people grew happy. With her subjects her name is sainted and she is styled as *avatar* (incarnation of divinity).

In view of what has been said above, Ahilyabai, along with many many other Hindu heroins, such as Rani of Jhansi, of course, but also Ranu Kittur Chennama or Tarabai, was a true Hindu heroine that incarnated early Hindu Power.

CHAPTER 13

True Hindu Heroes and Heroines: Maharana Pratap

The founder of present-day Udaipur, in Rajasthan, Udai Singh, was blessed with a son, Pratap, on May 9, 1540 at Kumbhalgarh, where it created all round rejoicing. The birth of Pratap proved very auspicious for his father Udai Singh: soon after, he could capture the famous Chittor fort, after defeating Banbeer at Mavoli. Thus, Udai Singh became the ruler of the entire Mewar and transferred his headquarters to Chittor. Pratap along with his mother, Jayanti Bai, also joined Udai Singh at Chittor. Here Jayanti Bai fully concentrated her attention towards the upbringing of his son. Being the heir apparent of Mewar, she tried her best to prepare Pratap for the future. In his early childhood, Jayanti Bai used to tell him the stories pertaining to the achievements of Pratap's ancestors. When he came of age, he was given the training in arms riding and all of warfare.

Besides it, he was also taught about the various aspects of administrative affairs. Pratap soon became adopt in handling weapons, so much so that at the age of fourteen, he was entrusted the command of the army and sent against Dungarpur in 1554. Grand success was achieved by Pratap and Askaran of Dungarpur had to accept the suzerainty of Mewar. The way he handled the entire campaign, formed a deep impression on the army. His brilliant success in different campaigns established a deep faith in his leadership amongst all section of society in Mewar. He also became acquainted with common people in general and tribal people in particular. He developed so much intimate relationship with them that Bhils used to call him 'kika' which means a 'son'. This bond of affection which subsisted between Pratap and tribal as well as common people of Mewar was a service of great strength for Pratap in his war against Mughals in future.

Mewar hitherto relied on the impregnable forts for its defense. But with the introduction of cannons, these forts lost their utility. Hence Udai Singh, wanted to shift his capital to suitable place to adapt to this new military strategy. With this in view in mind, he came to hilly tracks around present day Udaipur. During his search, he came across a sadhu, Premgiri, who advised him to lay the foundation at a particular spot, so that his kingdom would last for a long time. The Foundation of Udaipur was laid on April 15, 1553 A.D., which remained the capital of Mewar until today.

During this period significant events had been taking place in Northern India: the disintegration of the Sur empire, provided an opportunity for Mughals to revive their hold on Delhi. After the death of Moghul Emperor Humayun, his son Akbar became the emperor in 1556. His succession drastically changed the entire situation and being an ambitious monarch, Akbar could not tolerate the rebellious independence of Mewar.

Thus, in 1567, he marched against Mewar and reached Chittor, when it was still the capital, on October 23. Maharana Udai Singh, entrusted the defense of the fort to Jaimal and Patta, two great sons of Merta and Mewar respectively. The fort was heroically defended and garrison continued to offer gallant resistance for four months. But ultimately the fort fell to the hands of the enemy but not before every single person of the defenders had dedicated himself to death. All the princesses and common ladies threw themselves in an immense pyre to avoid being raped or taken as slaves by Akbar's soldiers. This is known as a 'Jauhar' and is remembered even today.

Thus, Akbar could capture Chittor on February 25, 1568. He stayed there for three days and ordered that thirty thousand of the civil Hindu population, be executed, including women and children who had taken shelter in the fort. Destruction of temples also took place on mass scale. This merciless massacre and destruction of temple was a great blot on Akbar who is regarded as the best of Moghul emperors.

The fall of Chittor, followed by the merciless destruction in the fort, demoralized the many important Rajput states of Rajasthan so that they accepted submission to the Mughals. However, Mewar continued its brave resistance against the whole force of the mighty emperor and refused to bow her head.

Udai Singh breathed his last on February 28, 1572 and Pratap inherited a very precarious throne: there was complete chaos in all spheres-political, economical, social etc. and the capital Chittor was already under the Mughals. The independence was an unacceptable challenge to then emperor Akbar. Soon after accession, Maharana Pratap sought the blessing of Mother India to free the country from the clutches of Melechas (Mughal). Not only this, but to boost the morale of his people and show his determination for the cause, he publicly renounced all types of material comforts, till his mother land was freed from the clutches of slavery.

At first, Akbar tried through persuasion to solve the problem: he sent four missions of peace to Pratap in the course of one year (1572-73) as the three first ones failed, he deputed one of his close generals, Man Singh, to Pratap, hoping that a Hindu could convince another Hindu. But this one also failed – war became therefore inevitable.

Maharana found an unexpected ally in Hakim Khan Sur, an Afghan and was able to gather many other Muslim soldiers and generals. At the same time Akbar continued to make efforts to isolate Pratap from his Rajput allies. He began to purchase horses and other war material at exorbitant prices, so that Pratap could not procure them. Still Arab traders came to Mewar with their horses to sell to Pratap

In the second week of March 1576, the emperor came to Ajmer and dispatched from there an army against Mewar under the command of Man Singh, along with many high-ranking Mughal officials.

In the ensuring months there were many troops movements and observing each other and Man Singh try to subdue Pratap through a scorched earth policy, but without success.

Both the armies came face to face on June 18, 1576. The battle is known as the battle of Haldighati. The pass got its name because of the turmeric colored soil around it. This pass was so narrow that only two persons could walk abreast across it with difficulty. It was even arduous for horses to gallop through it, and it was impossible for a horse to turn back with a rider.

Pratap divided his army into two divisions: besides Bhil tribesmen placed on the cliffs of the hills on both sides of the pass, he posted Hashim Khan Sur and as a general on the flanks. The attack by Pratap's army was so sudden and effective that the advance body of the Mughals sustained a complete defeat. Badayuni, a prominent Mughal historian present there admits that: "Hakim's attack shattered the defense line of the Mughals and the Rajputs of our army." There was a complete confusion in the Mughal army and it became difficult for them to make distinction between friendly Rajput and enemy Rajput. The force and rapidity with which the charge was made by the second division led by Pratap could be imagined by the fact that the Shahjadas of Sikri, Mansur, Gajikhan etc. ran away with their contingents – Badayuni also agrees that "those of the army who had fled on the first attack did not stop till they had passed by five or six kosh (15 to 20 k.m.) beyond the river."

During the battle, an encounter between Pratap, riding on his famous horse Chetak and Man Singh, also took place. According to Amar Kavya and other literary works, "Chetak jumped like a hungry tiger on the head of Man Singh's elephant and Pratap hurled his heavy spear at the Mughal General." Man Singh saved himself by dodging with a quick reflex action. The spear pierced the Mahawat. At this time Chetak received a cut in one of his forelegs. This action of Pratap attracted the attention of some of Man Singh's personal bodyguards who began to attack Pratap. But he not only parried the powerful strokes of sword made by sturdy Bahlol Khan Pathan but tore the torso of the armored Pathan along with his coat of mail into two.

It created confusion amongst the Mughal, taking advantage of it, both the divisions of Maharana's army reunited and left the ground to enter the narrow defile behind the hills. It was Maharana's strategy to trap the Mughals here, if they chose to pursue, but they did not pursue and the battle came to an end by midday.

The significance of the battle lies in this fact that the Mughals for the first time in fifty years could not overpower the Rajputs. In fact, this battle shattered the myth that the Mughals were unconquerable.

Maharana Pratap, a true Hindu hero, inspired the masses with his ideals. Every person of his state thus became a soldier for independence. It is surprising that inspite of all temptations from the Mughals, we do not come across any solitary case of any person deserting Pratap during these conflicts. The guerrilla war tactics were adopted so effectively that Pratap emerged victorious in post Haldighati period also. However, Pratap could not enjoy peace for long. During a hunting expedition, while striking his bow, Pratap received an injury on his body. It caused serious illness and every effort failed to recover Pratap from it. Ultimately Pratap succumbed to injury and passed away on January 19, 1597 at Chawand.

Maharana Pratap was great in peace as well in war. He became a legend during his lifetime and he forever would be considered as a great pioneer of the freedom movement in his country. As a torch bearer of liberty, he would continue to inspire millions of people in this land for all times to come. It is a pity that today this great Hindu hero is not known outside Rajasthan and some of the northern states and does not find pride of place in history books.

Chapter 14

True Hindu Heroes and Heroines: Sri Aurobindo

The Congress always claimed kinship and ownership to the 'Father of the Nation'. Is indeed the Mahatma, whose tremendous personality nobody can deny, the true architect of Indian Independence, as most history books, both Indian and western, are claiming?

Recent biographies of Sri Aurobindo, shed new light about Sri Aurobindo's role as a leader of the Congress. Not many people know that originally the Congress was created in December 1885 by an Englishman, A.O. Hume, with the avowed aim to: "Allow all those who work for the national (read British) good to meet each other personally."

Sri Aurobindo, however, was very clear in what was demanded then and today of a leader of India: "What India needs at the moment is the aggressive virtues, the spirit of soaring idealism, bold creation, fearless resistance, courageous attack." How many Indian politicians today fit into that mould, except for Narendra Modi?

Nirdodbaran one of his close disciples, recounts how Sri Aurobindo re-enacted five thousand years later, Krishna's message to Arjuna, by allowing his brother Barin to manufacture bombs in his own house and secretly endorsed early assassinations of select Englishmen. "He never ceased to believe that Indians had the right to use violence to topple a government maintained by violence." But how does that tally with the idea we have about spirituality, which we basically associate with non-violence? Hence this enormously important aspect of Sri Aurobindo's life, of protecting the Dharma, of standing for what is good and true and noble, by force, if necessary, is today ignored and not applied to the enemies of modern India. Sri Aurobindo is truly the father of Hindu Power.

In his famous Uttarpara speech, Sri Aurobindo, after one year in the Alipore jail, clearly defines what he calls the Sanatana Dharma: "Something has been shown to you in this year of seclusion, something about which you had your doubts and it is the truth of the Hindu religion. It is this religion that I am raising up before the world, it is this that I have perfected and developed through the rishis, saints and avatars, and now it is going forth to do my work among the nations. I am raising this nation to send forth my word... When therefore it is said that India shall rise, it is the Santana Dharma that shall rise. When it is said that India shall be great, it is the Santana Dharma that shall be great."

If we in France had a great man, such as Sri Aurobindo, who comes out in Nirodbaran's biography not only as a revolutionary, a yogi, but also a tremendous philosopher and a peerless poet, we would cherish him endlessly. His poetry would be taught to children, his philosophical works would be part of the universities curriculum, books would be written about him, museums built....

But today amongst Indian politicians, everybody quotes conveniently from Gandhi, although nobody applies his ideals of chakra, non-violence, khadi and chakra. Nobody ever mentions Sri Aurobindo, whose sayings of a 100 years ago are still 100% relevant today. Not only is he absent from schools and universities, but in some manuals written by the Congress, he is branded as a 'terrorist'. Shame on India!

The defunct Somnath Chaterjee, who was made an icon by the Media, in spite of having disobeyed his party and sitting on the cash for votes scam, has built an Indian History museum in the Parliament annexe at a great cost of the tax payer's money. In this museum, which is visited by all school children of Delhi and surrounding states, the history of India more or less starts with Ashoka (because he was supposedly Buddhist), jumps to Akbar (who is glorified beyond measure) and finishes up with Subash Chandra Bose, Gandhi and

Nehru. Not a single mention of Sri Aurobindo or even Tilak, the true fathers of the nation.

Is it not time that Indian history be rewritten and rectify the major injustice done to Sri Aurobindo, Tilak and a few early revolutionaries, as the true fathers of Indian Independence, he who prophetically said about Pakistan in 1947: “India is free, but she has not achieved unity, only a fissured and broken freedom... The whole communal division into Hindu and Muslim seems to have hardened into the figure of a permanent political division of the country. It is to be hoped that the Congress and the Nation will not accept the settled fact as for ever settled, or as anything more than a temporary expedient. For if it lasts, India may be seriously weakened, even crippled; civil strife may remain always possible, possible even a new invasion and foreign conquest. The partition of the country must go... For without it the destiny of India might be seriously impaired and frustrated. That must not be.”

CHAPTER 15

Hindu Power: Islamophobia and Hinduphobia

We hear more and more in the world today that there is increased Islamophobia. The American media, particularly CNN or the New York Times, have been going all guns blazing out against Islamophobia. and generally, ethnic intolerance.

But the question arises: is there really Islamophobia? Well, it is a cliché, because it has been repeated so many times, yet from a statistical point of view, it is an undeniable fact: 90% of terrorist acts in the world in the last 40 years, from the time of Arafat, have been performed by Muslims. It is also a fact that the silent Muslim majority of the world, on the one hand never protests collectively the horrifying murders that have done in the name of the Koran; and on the other, secretly justifies in their minds these terrorist acts in the name of Palestine, Chechnya or Kashmir. It could also be said that according to Buddhist philosophy as the Dalai lama today expresses it, that there is also a collective karma for nations: "Tibetans, he says, are paying today, a black karma they incurred by their clinging to a feudal system for centuries." Thus, in the Buddhist perspective, Muslims may be reborn Muslims from life to life; for the untold atrocities committed in the name of Islam unto nations they conquered in the Middle Ages particularly against Hindus. Hence from this angle, every Muslim in the world should feel responsible for what is done in the name of Islam.

Quite a few Muslims have already stated it: the Koran was written for the people of the Middle Ages and was alright for these times, but now that we are in the 21st century, it needs to be reformed, as some of these passages which deal with infidels, with physical jihad, with women, which conversion to Islam, that once where all right, are used to the letter by Islamic terrorism to kill innocent people. Western Christianity (not the one practiced in India), has shown the path: in the 21st-century Christians acknowledged the facts that there are other religions and that it is necessary for a peaceful world to accept them. A Christian today is able to come to India and enter a Hindu temple without feeling that he or she is committing a sin. However we can safely say that at the moment's no Muslim authority is ready to change the Koran. Thus the on going war between Islam and the Western world along with India – and eventually with China, as it is facing also a problem with its own Muslim minority – will last quite some time.

This will trigger a phenomenon that we can witness already, though still in a small trickle: Muslims quietly leaving Islam, as they find it difficult to hire a flat, find schools for their children, apply for a job or simply because of facing discrimination in their lives. Other Muslims will cry of Islamophobia – but they should look within themselves and understand that collectively each Muslim is accountable for the crimes committed in the name of the Koran. Intellectuals and much of the media as CNN in the United States, The Guardian in UK, or Le Monde in Paris, who will continue to defend Muslims, should realize that it would be much more helpful if they would report the truth as it is: that Islam cannot win a war against the entire civilised world and that it would be better if the Koran is adapted to modern times so that Muslims can continue to have a peaceful life.

In India we have observed something called Hinduphobia. It is there in the Media, its there amongst intellectuals. While there is in the media strong defence of Muslims human rights – the life of a Hindu does not seem to count for much. I personally witnessed this in Kashmir specially in the 90s, when the entire foreign media was there, including famous journalists, such as Mark Tully. They all reported human rights abuses by the Army against Kashmiri Muslims, but when Hindu leaders started being murdered by what was then the KLF, and 350,000 Kashmiri Hindus later fled their ancestral land and houses without firing a shot in self-defence, becoming refugees in their own country, none of them gave a damn – and that is still true today. Hinduphobia resides also in the fact that when a Christian is killed, for instance quite a few years ago the horrible murder of the Australian missionary Graham Staines, who was burnt alive along his two young sons, or the killing of the innocent Muslim, suspected of having cow smuggling, more recently, you will notice an immediate uproar in the media. Whereas the killing of Hindu, especially if he is of the RSS of the BJP, as it happens frequently nowadays in Kerala, or West Bengal, hardly finds any mention in newspapers and televisions. And this triggers an important question – is the life of a Muslim or a Christian infinitely more important to the media than that of a Hindu?

Another form of Hinduphobia is the intense dislike that the media has for Hindu political leaders and Hindu political or social parties. This is particularly true of the RSS, an organisation that has been demonised first by the British and then today by the media and the politicians. When I started working as a journalist in India I had heard about the 'evil' RSS, and thus I was quite surprised when I went to interview their chief in their Delhi quarters, to find that they all looked like old fuddy-duddies in their oversize brown shorts. It was never really proved that Nathuram Ghose killed the Mahatma Gandhi on the orders of the RSS, yet this accusation is still being used on and on again, specially by the Congress party to paint them evil and even ban them. Nearer to us, we witness how Narendra Modi was also demonised (see later chapter) by the leftist Indian intellectuals as well as the media. The Hinduphobia against Narendra Modi went to such an extent that Sonia Gandhi would not have minded him killed, when bombs were planted at one of the 2014 electoral rallies in Patna, Bihar.

In conclusion, if there is some justification to Islamophobia, **there is none to Hinduphobia.** Let us repeat it again: Hindus have been the most tolerant people in the world, yet this has been a one-way traffic: Hindus have been the most persecuted people in the word, they have been invaded and colonised by many nations, from Alexander the Great to the Moghols and every European nation took its pound of gold and flesh. The sad thing is that today Western and Indian intellectuals, as well as Western and Indian media still stand up for Islam, however many crimes are committed in its name – and invariably go after Hindus.

CHAPTER 16

Hindu Power and Western Media Hatred

When India's space agency *ISRO* launched its first mission to Mars, prior to the *103* satellites sent later, the New York Times ran a demeaning cartoon, showing an Indian farmer with his cow, knocking at the doors of the Elite Space Club...

And this triggers an important question: 70 years after Independence, are western journalists and correspondents still biased against India (and Hindus), a country they are supposed to report honestly about, so that their readers, who are mostly ignorant, get enlightened?

Well, from a western correspondent himself, the answer is.. YES...

There are four reasons for that sad fact:

(1) India is never in the news in the West, unless there is some major catastrophe, or huge elections. Thus, if you want to write and be published, you have to find alternate stories, that often border on the sensational, the marginal, or even the untruthful...

(2) Your editor in New York, Paris or London, has often set ideas on India, even though most of the time he or she has never set foot here. You need to toe the line, otherwise you may not be published, which is tough if you are a freelance, that is paid per piece. Most western correspondents thus rein in. I had one guy like that in Paris, Charles Lambroschini, in LeFigaro.fr, who believed that the RSS was the most dangerous outfit in India...

(3) Three, or even five years, which is the usual period that foreign correspondents are posted (as well as diplomats) is *not enough* for understanding a country that is so vast, so diverse, so contradictory sometimes. In fact one needs to go beyond the appearances in India. Indeed, the western sense of the hygienic and the esthetical, is very different from India's and the first contact of dirtiness, slums, or poverty, often scars the perception of many western correspondents who then refused to go beyond that barrier.

(4) Delhi, where everybody is posted, is physically so far from the rest of India, and so disconnected. The same ideas and clichés are heard in parties and embassies' cocktails and repeated ad infinitum, till every foreign correspondent thinks they are the gospel truth: 'secularism, minorities, Hindu fundamentalism, human rights in Kashmir, right wing saffron' etc...

Is this why CNN or the New York Times, or the Independent, have been particularly nasty in the last few years against the BJP and Narendra Modi, even after he was democratically elected twice by 600 million Indians? It feels more like a biased witch-hunt than actual reporting. The antagonism that recently greeted the removal of Article 370 by Modi, was also an ignorant hostility, not based on facts – like Kashmir divided in three parts, with a Buddhist majority in Ladakh and a Hindu one in Jammu, or the Valley of Kashmir, having had a million Hindus at beginning of 20th century – and none today, as they were all chased by Islamic terror...

But the pioneer of them all has got to be the BBC, which has been the inspiration of much of the slant of the foreign journalists towards India, which seems to stem from an unconscious sense of superiority (same is true of western Indologists). The sad fact is that most of the Indian stringers of major western media outlets, such as BBC, or AP, or CNN, toe the line, that is report what their masters want them to say. In fact they go sometimes even overboard, to paint a negative and clichéd image of their own country. No doubt the Nirbhaya rape was a horrible happening and the guilty should have been punished in a harsher manner (and not released, like the so-called juvenile). But this was so much reported on, so much hyped, particularly by the BBC, that every westerner thinks now that India is the land of rape. In fact when any western girl wants to travel to India now, she is warned, "careful – you might be raped." Yet proportionately there are less rapes in India than in Sweden, which has the maximum number of rapes in the world, for instance and it is safer to walk at night in Delhi than in certain suburbs of Washington or Paris.

India should have a look at China, which gets a lot more respect from western journalists. Why? Because China does not take insults lying down. Paradoxically, western journalists have so much more liberty in India, where they can move freely. Whereas in China, they still need permission before going anywhere and need to submit the subject of their reporting. They can be censored too, or their websites even blocked.

Sure, there is no conspiracy that I can see, and most western correspondents come to India with a sincere aspiration to report fairly and faithfully. But again, the first task of a foreign journalist, without being blind to India's faults – and there are many, but not more than any other country in the world – should be to report truthfully and create some empathy amongst its readers or viewers for a country that is unique and endearing and whose ancient civilization, that viewed the world as One Family, has survived centuries of savage onslaught, including by the British, who are still trying to lecture India.

CHAPTER 17

The Western Media's Hatred against Narendra Modi

India is so different from the West, full of contradictions, paradoxes, baffling parameters, etc. Thus, for Westerners, who share more or less the same religion (Christianity), more or less the same ethnic origins (Caucasian), more or less the same food habits (meat) and more or less the same dress code (ties and dresses), India can be a very enigmatic country.

The New York Times has been particularly biased against Hindus and their political leaders, Firstly, the usual dislike, which borders on hatred, for Hindu politicians, comes out strongly in their portrayal of Narendra Modi, even after he was named as the BJP's official candidate in 2014 and 2019, even though he had, after all, made of his state, Gujarat, the most efficient, most prosperous and least corrupt of all the states of India. Of course, they label – and still do – Modi "anti-Muslim and accuse him of having engineered the 2002 Gujarat anti-Muslim riots, carefully omitting the fact that they were triggered by the horrifying murder of 57 Hindus, 36 of them innocent women and children, burnt like animals in the Sabarmati Express. Riots of that intensity like in Gujarat, do not happen in a day, they are a result of long term pent-up angers and a spark like the killing of Hindu brothers and sisters, whose only crime was that they believed that Ram was born in Ayodhya, is enough the ignite the smouldering fire.

Of course the New York Times choses also to demonize Hindus, implying that the "roughly 80% Hindu Population" (Hindus are much less today) are ostracizing the 13% Muslim population (who are much more now with the Bangladesh influx (I would say near 20%) and that Modi used the inherent Hindu nationalist streak in every Hindu to be re-elected Prime Minister in 2019 with the blood and tears of Muslims (he did get re-elected and it is said that he got quite a few Muslim votes).

As we keep emphasizing, you cannot find anybody less fundamentalist than a Hindu in the world. However today, Hindus are still being targeted: in the last 20 years. Hindus, the overwhelming majority community of this country, are being made fun of, are despised, are deprived of the most basic facilities for one of their most sacred pilgrimages in Amarnath while their government heavily sponsors the Haj. They see their brothers and sisters converted to Christianity through inducements and financial traps, and their gods are blasphemed.

Let us repeat again: there are about a billion Hindus, one in every six persons on this planet. They form one of the most successful, law-abiding and integrated communities in the world today – see how well they integrated in the United States, never giving problems to the US government, paying their taxes, topping in universities and today grabbing some of the top jobs of the country. Can the New York Times ignore that and the fact that Narendra Modi may be their spokesperson?

CHAPTER 18

Hinduphobia: Mocking Hindus, their Politicians and Gurus

It is sad that the Supreme Court again opened the case of the Babri Masjid's against LK Advani and Murli Manohar Joshi. I have known these two men for more than 30 years. Mr Advani is an upright, honest, dedicated and non-corrupt politician, who has been labelled all kinds of names by the Media. Yet, I have never seen him ask anything for himself or his family and he always lived a simple life. Indeed, his Spartan habits have carried him to an advanced age, where he still has all his physical and mental abilities.

Politics is something of a Russian Roulette: sometimes you win, sometimes you lose. There is no doubt that Advani would have made a good Prime Minister. But Vajpayee always kept him in check, and when Modi came on the scene, Advani was already in his 80s. This is why I would have liked to see Advani as the President of India, for he would have been an honourable, active and pro-India one. But it's too late now. I want to here pay my respects to Ms Advani and Joshi, because 30 years ago, when it was not fashionable, they were pioneers of Hindu Power and led the way for the coming of the BJP and Narendra Modi to form this strong Government that is now spreading its wings all over India. The BJP4India owes them a lot, and in true Indian traditions, it should honour them, as elders have always been honoured in India. I thought then that these two men had courage and dedication and this is why I always stood by them in my writings.

These habits of the media to debase its Hindu politicians, also applies to Hindu gurus. As the great actor Vinod Khanna who passed away, one of the most intelligent and creative Bollywood players, we recall that he also had the courage to give up everything, fame and wealth, to follow his Guru Osho. Who remembers today that Osho was the target of ridicule by Indian journalists, that he had to flee to the United States, where there he was also hounded and even thrown in jail. But for sure, he is not the only Hindu Guru hassled in India. Maharishi Yogi also left his native country, as he was persecuted and took refuge in Holland. Sai Baba one of the great gurus of the 21st century, was beleaguered relentlessly by the media. And so are many other gurus who have also been ridiculed or pursued by the Media and Indian Intelligentsia. It is thus no mystery that many gurus even went to jail. We think about the Shankaracharya, who spent quite many months in prison, without ever been charged, or even today Asaram Bapu, who is still in jail.

The Intelligentsia, the NGO's and the media also went out all guns blazing against Sri Sri Ravi Shankar for his 2016 World Cultural Festival, which gathered 3 million people in Delhi the capital, coming from all over the world, and bringing precious foreign exchange to the government. Sri Sri is supposed to have damaged the fragile Yamuna ecological system, but everyone who lives nearby knows that it is mostly a sewer, that stinks to heaven and that not much can survive in its black waters, even jungle fish. The irony is that Sri Sri is the only one that tried to do something for the Yamuna river when a few years ago, thousands of his volunteers embarked upon a project to clean it. I was there. Yet the National Green Tribunal, whom we never heard before and who did not do much to clean India's damaged ecology, its rivers and forests, did a witch hunt on the Art of Living.

Why is it that the intellectuals, the NGOs and the journalists always go after Hindus, their politicians and their gurus? Well, firstly, Hindus have always taken insults lying down, that is they hardly react to them – not like Muslims, who, if you say anything about the Prophet or the Koran, go down in the streets and riot, or even kill. Then, Hindus however many wonderful qualities they have, are a very very disunited lot, as we have seen earlier, either out of selfishness, or because Hinduism is too much of an individualistic religion. Finally, it is actually the British, who, when they were masters of India, started in their newspapers to make fun of the Hindus and their customs, derided cow worship and Hindu pujas, or always harped on the 'evil' caste system. Is it not then that today's Indian journalists are true children of the British, who planted in their forefathers the seeds of Hinduphobia?

Furthermore, it must be said that Nehru, the first Prime Minister of India, adopted at Independence a socialism that was heavily inspired from the Soviet Union. He felt that this socialism was the best way to level all the inequalities, social, economical, and of caste, that were then prevalent in India. He also had to deal with an important Muslim minority that had chosen to stay in India and not join Pakistan. It is for these two reasons that he asked his historians to prop-up Muslim rulers such as Akbar or even the terrible Aurangzeb and denied the greatness of Hindu warriors such as Shivaji Mahjaraj or Maharana Pratap, knowing that Hindus would stay quiet.

Nehru also pampered Christians and Muslims, giving them not only freedom of worship, which Hindus do not get in Pakistan or Gulf countries, but also allowed them total control of their places of worship; whereas the government took over most Hindu temples. He also fashioned a generation of scholars, intellectuals, journalists and even NGO workers, that looked down upon Hinduism as a religion that was backwards and would brake India's economy growth. Indeed one remembers his famous quote: "Dams are the new temples of India."

Hinduphobia thus attained a peak that even the British had not dreamed off under Nehru and continues to rule today as subsequent nehruvian generations, in schools, universities, families, either bred total ignorance about Hinduism, or outright contempt. This is why today we find that the media always attacks or mocks Hindus, their gurus or even their politicians. Let us hope that Narendra Modi, in his second term, will effect in India a tremendous transformation, that will recognise that not only Hindus have the overwhelming majority in this country, but that Hinduism is the only religion today that accepts and respects all the other religions of the world, including Islam.

Hindu gurus are one of the most ancient and sacred traditions of this land and the media should at least respect that, so that western correspondents posted in Delhi, take notice and pay a little more respect to Hindus, who are the descendants of one of the most ancient and wisest civilisations of our History.

CHAPTER 19

Sonia Gandhi, the Empress of Hinduphobia

Like Sonia Gandhi, I am a Westerner and a brought-up catholic. My father, a very good man, was a staunch Christian; my uncle, whom I doted upon, was the vicar of the Montmartre Church, one of the most picturesque landmarks of Paris. Like Sonia Gandhi, I have lived in India for more than 50 years, and I have had the good fortune to be married to an Indian.

But the comparison stops there. I did land in India with a certain amount of prejudices, clichés and false ideas, that most Westerners pick-up here and there (Tintin, Kipling, the City of Joy, Slumdog Millionaire, today) and I did think in the enthusiasm of my youth to become a missionary to bring back Indian 'pagans' to the 'true God'. But the moment I stepped in India I felt that not only I had nothing much that I could give to India, but rather, that it was India which was bestowing me. In fact, in 50 years, India has given me so much, professionally, spiritually, sentimentally. Most Westerners, who come here, still think they are here to 'give' something to a country, which, unconsciously of course, they think is lesser than theirs. It was true of the British, it was true of Mother Teresa, it is true today of Mrs Sonia Gandhi.

It is a fact that Sonia brought some discipline, order and cohesion into the Congress party. But the amount of power, that she, a non-Indian, a simple elected MP, like hundreds of others, possessed when the Congress was in power for two long terms, before Mr Modi came, should have frightened her. Her power was indeed terrifying: a word, nay a glance of her was sufficient to trigger action by her entourage, using any means, like the forced removal of Baba Ramdev from Delhi. Thus, the instruments of power were never so perverted in India. The CBI blatantly and shamelessly quashed all injunctions against Quattrochi and even allowed him to get away with billions of rupees which he had stolen from India. Yet, without batting an eyelid, and with the Indian Media turning a blind eye, she went ruthlessly after the Chief Minister of the most efficiently run state, the most corruption free, who later became the very Prime Minister of India, using any dirty means to throw him into jail, as well as his Interior minister Amit Shah. In those times the Congress, with Sonia's overt or silent consent, paid crores of rupees to buy MP's to topple non-Congress state governments. Her governors shamelessly hijacked democracy by twisting the laws.

Were Indians aware that their country had entered then a state of semi-autocracy, where every important decision came to a single individual, as recent files released by the New Indian Express have shown, residing in her fortress of Janpath, surrounded by dozens of security men, an empress of India. Are Indians aware that she controlled – and still does – tens of billions of rupees of the taxpayer's money, which she used to keep her party in power? Did they know that the huge amounts of the scams, whether the 2G, the CWG, or the Adarsh one, did not go into politicians pockets (only a fraction), but to the coffers of the Congress for the next general elections, which they lost thank God, and more than anything to please Sonia?

Nobody seemed to notice what was happening under the reign of Sonia Gandhi. That an Arundhati Roy was allowed to preach secession in India, whereas on the other hand the Congress Government has been going after the army, the last body in India to uphold the time honoured values of the Kshatriya – courage, honour, devotion to the Motherland, they who alone today practice true secularism, never differentiating between a Muslim or Hindu soldier, and who, for a pittance, give daily their lives to their country. First it was the attempt of a caste census, a divide and rule ploy if there is one; then there were the first signs that the Government was thinking about thinning down the presence of the Indian army in the Kashmir Valley, which would have suited Pakistan perfectly. And then there was the Adarsh scam, in which the army officers, at the worst, were innocently dragged into it. We know now that it was the politicians of the Congress who benefited the most of it.

One hears from persons who know her well, of Sonia's' qualities of honesty, courtesy, or personal care. But would be impossible, in France for example, to have a non-Christian, say an Hindu for instance, who is a non-elected president or PM, to be the absolute ruler of the country behind the scenes, superseding even the PM. There are many capable people in the Congress. Why can't a billion Indians find one of their own, who will understand the complexity and subtlety of India, to govern themselves? Not only that, but her very presence at the top had and still unleashes forces, visible and invisible, that are detrimental to the country. There is nothing wrong in espousing the best of the values of the West – democracy, technological perfection, higher standards of living – but many of the institutions are crumbling in the West: two out of three marriages end in divorce, kids shoot each other, parents are not cared for in their old age, depression is rampant and westerners are actually looking for answers elsewhere, in India notably.

One does not understand this craze she had with the Congress to westernize India at all costs, while discarding its ancient values. Mrs Gandhi should do well to remember that there still are 850 million Hindus in India, a billion worldwide and that whatever good inputs were brought by different invasions, it is the ancient values of the spirituality behind Hinduism, which have made India so special and which gives her today her unique qualities. It was an insult to these tolerant Hindus to show President Obama as his first input of the Indian capital the tomb of Humayun, a man who slaughtered Hindus in thousands, taking Hindu women and children as captives. He even subjected his elder brother Kamran to brutal torture, gauging his eyes out and pouring lemon into them.

The tragedy of India is that it was colonized for too long. And unlike China, it always looks to the West for a solution to its problems. Sonia Gandhi, whatever her qualities, is just an incarnation of that hangover, an Empress of India in new clothes.

Chapter 20

Hinduphobia against Brahmins and other Upper Castes

It is true that the Congress only took over from the British the art of divisive politics, which is to polarize India on castes and religions: "I am a Muslim first and then an Indian"; "I am a Dalit first and then an Indian"; "I am a Christian first and then and Indian"... Even Mayawati, before CM Yogi was elected, wanted Brahmins, who have, whatever their faults, shown patriotism throughout Indian history (hello Mangal Pandey), to say: "I am a Brahmin first and then an Indian." Today the Congress wishes us to believe all these caste reservations and pandering to the Muslims is done to elevate minorities; but in truth it is just a cynical arithmetic computation: with the votes of the Dalits and the Muslims, anybody can be elected. It is true that the Congress got bashed-up in UP, in the last general elections, but is equally true that Mayawati upped them with the same calculation, adding a peppering of upper castes for good effect...

There is also a perversion of statistics and facts. Yes, there are still terrible inequalities in India, extremely rich people and the poorest of the poor. Yes, there are Dalits who are oppressed. But no country in the world has done so much for its underprivileged since 1947. Today, many government academic, bureaucratic and even medical posts in India are held by Dalits and OBC. A Harijan made it to the highest post of President, and India had another two Muslims as Presidents, a Sikh as PM and a Christian as Its 'Eminence Grise'. Did France ever boast of a Muslim Prime Minister, or a Hindu President? No way – and it will take a long time to happen.

In fact today, it is the Brahmins who have become the Dalits of India. Brahmins are in minority in most of the UP villages, where Dalits constitute 60 to 65%; most of the intellectual Brahmin Tamil class has emigrated outside Tamil Nadu; the average income of Brahmins is less than that of non-Brahmins; a high percentage of Brahmin students drop out at the intermediate level ; 75% of domestic help and cooks in Andhra Pradesh are Brahmins; and most of Delhi's public toilets are cleaned by Brahmins (see stats below). Yet, contrary to the West, where Christian priests and popes constantly meddled in politics and acquired huge health and land, which led to the separation of the Church and the State under the French revolution, the much maligned Brahmins never interfered in affairs of state throughout Indian history, restraining themselves to advising kings and maharajas on spiritual matters.

Dalits should never forget that castes, which once upon a time was just a an arrangement for the distribution of functions in society, just as much as class in Europe, has been the stick that all invaders have used to put down India - and it is today still skillfully employed by missionaries and Marxists (and the millions of parasite NGO's who make money out of India's misery, without really uplifting anything but their own bank accounts, one of the greatest scams today). On top of that, nowadays, it is not the Brahmins who oppress the Dalits, but the OBC. See many villages in Tamil Nadu: Dalits are parked in one corner and cannot enter the area devoted to Vanniars, who are just one rung above them.

Is the casteisation of politics in India, as it is still embodied in some parts of UP and Bihar, here to stay? We hope not, as it may lead to the balkanization of India. What is the key to stem this rot? Education. Many Indians do not feel nationalistic enough (except for cricket, the lowest and most worthless denomination of nationalism) and put their castes and religions forward, because they are not groomed in school to be proud to be Indians. As a result, the IMM's and IIT's just produce brilliant clones, without any root in their culture, who export themselves to the West to stay there. It also produces generation after generation of Indians, who scorn on their own culture and look-up to the West and some of the values like materialism and Marxism, which have failed there. But if right after kindergarten, you would teach children about the greatness of their culture, a little bit of the good of each religion, great poets, saints and epics such as the Mahabharata, which is a universal Scripture, one would produce generation after generation of true Indians.

The hate against Brahmins first shown by the Muslim invaders, then by the British and today espoused by Christian missionaries, Indian Marxists and much of the Indian intelligentsia, is too strongly imbedded in the collective psyche. They should remember Mayawati and her mentor Kanshi Ram's early war cry: *Tilak, taraju aur talwar, unko maro juthe char* ('Brahmins, traders and the warrior caste should be kicked'). Look also at what happened to the four hundred thousand Brahmins of Kashmir who fled though terror their homeland without raising a little finger in defense. Today no political party gives a damn about them and many of them are still languishing in refugee camps – in their own country – a first in the sad history of Humanity.

You knew about OBC, Other Backward Castes, now you have to learn about "O.U.C"., 'Other Upper Castes', a term coined by an obscure bureaucrat from the Home Ministry. Do you know that Brahmins and OUC, according to the National Sample Survey's (NSS) report, comprise 36% of India, a huge bank vote which ignores its own power? And are the Brahmins and OUC aware that together they may constitute more than the OBC's vote bank, if one excludes SC and ST, which constitute 13% of the 52% Mandal OBC list? There are further post 1931 caste census adjustments to be made, due to the merger of Rajput Dominated Princely States with rest of India, which took of 4%; and another 4% due to migration at the time of Partition. Thus, we come to an OBC actual population, All Religions Taken, excluding ST and ST of 22.5%.

People think that Brahmins and OUC are rich, arrogant and cut off from society. Are you aware that today Brahmins and OUC work as toilet cleaners, coolies, rickshaw pullers, that temple priests sometimes earn less than 350 Rs a month? But what about the

Thakurs, the farmers and landlords, who have such a bad reputation in Bihar and UP, as having huge lands and exploiting the lower castes? A paper by D. Narayana, Centre for Development Studies, Thiruvanantpuram ("Perception, Poverty and Health: A Contribution" CICRED Seminar on Poverty and Health, Feb. 2005), shows that 69.8% of Brahmins and OUC never went past 12th standard, that 52,4% of Brahmins and OUC farmers don't owe land bigger than 100 cents, quite insufficient to nourish a family, and that that 53.9 % of the upper caste population is below poverty line. So much for the clichés and prejudices in India about Brahmins and Thakurs.

Narayana thus concludes: "Just as the higher ritual status of Brahmins does not necessarily translate into economic or political supremacy, those lower in the ranks are able to move up in the local hierarchy through the capture of political power, the acquisition of land, and migration to other regions. A combination of these strategies and India's policy of quotas or reservations have particularly benefited the so-called backward castes, or Shudras. Referred to as "other backward classes" (OBCs) in administrative parlance, backward castes are defined as those whose ritual rank and occupational status are above "untouchables" but who themselves remain socially and economically depressed. Contrary to the general presumption that the OBCs belong to the deprived sections of Hindu society, few groups in independent India have made progress on a scale comparable to the OBCs."

We are often told that Tamil Nadu is an example of successful reservations' policies. But the Dravidian movement's success has its origins in the anti-Brahmin movement launched in the first part of the 20th century. One century on, the DMK continues to stoke those feelings. Most of the Brahmins who once enlightened Tamil Nadu have now fled to other parts of India and abroad, probably one of the greatest migrations of intellectuals from any country in the world. It is true that thanks to reservation, social justice has returned to Tamil Nadu. But at what price? The only Brahmins left there are priests and the DMK, which will be probably back in power at the next state elections (with a Chief Minister named Stalin!), might also strip them of this last privilege. But it takes decades to master the art of Sanskrit and puja and priesthood today is not a very lucrative career, as many Pandits are wallowing in poverty. So how many takers will there be for their post? This is another empty vote bank posturing, which will split more India on caste lines.

I get huge amount of mails from Brahmins and OUC, grateful that someone has at last taken note of their plight, but also a few mails (3%) from people saying that we are anti Dalit. Firstly I would like to say that after so many years in India, particularly in the cities, I am still not able to see the difference between a Dalit and a Brahmin, except if I see a Brahmin wearing a sacred thread and a Dalit in a loincloth, which is never the case in cities. Secondly, we live partly in the South near Pondicherry, where most of the local inhabitants are Vanniars an OBC caste, just above the untouchables. I play basketball with them, our marriage witnesses were both Vanniars and our best friend there is a Tamil OBC. Thirdly as all Westerners (and French), I am revolted by social inequalities. When during the Tsunami in Pondicherry, Vanniars stopped Dalits (whose access to their burial ground had been flooded), from crossing their village to bury their dead, I was appalled. When in Benares during a recent survey, a few Brahmins tell us that they still will not let a Shudra enter their house, I am revolted and I think to myself that Brahmins deserve the treatment they are getting today.

Nevertheless, things have gone overboard: Nehru wanted that the Brahmins and OUC of yesterday became the Dalits of tomorrow and Sonia Gandhi completed his task at an alarming rate. Today the Hindus, the huge majority of this country, they whose culture is the backbone and the genius of India, with virtues of tolerance, spirituality, acceptance of all, are treated like a minority by the Congress and more and more ostracized. It may be true that chunks of India are still ruled by some of the erstwhile upper classes; but the 36% upper castes of India, the Brahmins, Thakurs, Vaishiyas, Jains, Marwahris, Baniyas (Guptas/goals etc.), are more and more marginalized, their voices are not heard, and their children have to emigrate abroad, because merit is not any more sufficient to get admission in a university or a Government job. When will this great brain drain stop? What a terrible loss for India. Not only Brahmins and OUC kept alive India's old age spirituality carried down throughout the ages, India's sacred texts, including the Bhaghavad Gita, humanity's Future Bible, but they are also some of the top most scientists, engineers, software people, writers, artists of this country...

Will this 36% so called upper castes forever remain disunited, silent, and see its role more and more diminished, India more and more Christianized, Islamized, de-hinducized, marxist-cized? This may be the dream of Sonia Gandhi, but that will spell the doom of the India we all love. Today, although outwardly many of the OUC still control parts of India there are many areas, such as bureaucracy, schools, universities, hospitals, where the backward classes, often without merit, exercise huge control. **We need an India based on merit not on caste**. Indians should feel Indians first and then belonging to that caste or that religion after.

O Brahmins and OUC, awake, not against the lower castes, who are your brothers and sisters and whom you did sometimes mistreat for centuries, but against cynical governments which try to divide India more and more along caste and religion lines. Let go of your centuries' old disunity and selfishness, and unite: the power is still with you.

* Brahmins of India by J. Radhakrishna, published by Chugh Publications, reveals that all purohits today live below the poverty line.
* 50% of the richshaw pullers in New Delhi's Patel Nagar are Brahmins.
* Only 9 seats out 600 in the combined UP and Bihar assembly are held by Brahmins – the rest are in the hands of the Yadavs.
* The last 400.000 Brahmins of the Kashmir valley, the once respected Kashmiri Pandits, now live as refugees in their own country.
* 75% of domestic help and cooks in Andhra Pradesh are Brahmins.

* In the 5-18 year age group, 44 per cent Brahmin students stopped education at the primary level and 36 per cent at the pre-matriculation level.
* Seventy percent of Brahmins are still relying on their hereditary vocation. There are hundreds of families that are surviving on just Rs. 300 per month as priests in various temples (*Department of Endowments* statistics).
* At Tamil Nadu's Ranganathaswamy Temple, a priest's monthly salary is Rs. 500 (Census Department studies) and a daily allowance of one measure of rice. The government staff at the same temples receive Rs.2500 plus per month.
* Brahmins and Other Upper Castes, according to the National Sample Survey's (NSS) 99 report, constitute 36% of India, a huge bank vote which ignores its own power.
* A paper by D. Narayana, Centre for Development Studies, Thiruvanantpuram ("Perception, Poverty and Health: A Contribution" CICRED Seminar on Poverty and Health, Feb. 2005), shows that

(1) 69.8% of Brahmins and Other Upper Castes never went past 12th standard.

(2) That 52.4% of Brahmins and OUC farmers don't owe land bigger than 100 cents, quite insufficient to nourish a family.

(3) And that that 53.9 % of the upper caste population is below poverty line.

Chapter 21

Hinduphobia and the Great Aryan Divide

Everything possible has been written in the last twenty years to try to explain how Congressmen, big and small, important and humble, have been humiliating and debasing themselves in front of Sonia Gandhi, time and time again, including when Rahul Gandhi resigned of the Presidency, after the Congress 2019 general elections debacle.

There is sycophancy, of course: it is an old Congress tradition, although it should be said that Indian sycophancy is a perverted offshoot of *bhakti*, the great Hindu tradition of worshipping "That" which seems to be above us, regardless of its value; there is obviously self-interest – most of the Congress bigwigs, who are much more intelligent that they are credited for, know that without Sonia (or Nehru / or Rajiv / or Indira), they stand to get very little votes; there is the dynasty rule angle - but again, dynasty is a very western word, which applies more to the American soap opera of the same name, than to India, where the concept of *bhakti*, coupled with the old *maharaja* tradition, have always ensured respects for "royal" families; there is the foreign angle, naturally: let us not forget that the Congress was founded by a Scot, A.O. Hume, and that for long it was manipulated by its British masters to ensure that India stayed with the Crown – with Sonia, another foreigner at its helm again, Congress has come a full circle; lastly, there is an element which has been overlooked: the *shakti* element, which is so strong and prevalent in India, that it allowed Indira Gandhi to govern with an iron hand this male-dominated country for nearly twenty years and that it has even survived in the neighbouring Islamic states, such as Pakistan or Bangladesh, witness Benazir Bhutto or the two Bangla Begums. But the main cause for this morbid fascination that Sonia Gandhi, whatever her merits exercises on Indians in general, whether they love or hate her, is the Great Myth of the Aryan Invasion of India....

... For a long time, it was known in Europe that it owed a lot of its culture, philosophy and science to ancient Vedic India. American mathematician A. Seinderberg has for instance proven than the Egyptians pyramids were built using ancient Vedic mathematics known as "Sulbasutras"; Egyptians considered that their God Osiris, whose concept is derived from one of the stories described in the Puranas, had come from India mounted on a bull (nandi). Greek philosophy, which is the founding stone for western Culture recognised that it hads borrowed heavily from India: German philosopher Shroeder had discovered in the 18th century that most of the philosophical or mathematical doctrines attributed to Pythagoras were derived from Indian philosophical systems. French historian Alain Danielou had noticed that the structure of the catholic church resembles that of Buddhist Chaitya and that many events surrounding the life of Christ are borrowed from Buddhist and Krishnaïtes stories. Nietzsche, who knew the Vedas and Manu's laws, is the last of Europe's great philosophers to speak highly "of the great tradition of Brahmanism". But after his death, the memory of a greater India slowly fades from philosophers' writings and history books and is replaced by a negation of India's great influence on the world. What has happened?

The first and foremost explanation for this forgetfulness could be the theorem of the *Aryan invasion*, which is still taken as the foundation stone of the History of India. According to this theory, which was actually devised in the 18th and 19th century by British linguists and archaeologists, who had a vested interest to prove the supremacy of their culture over the one of the subcontinent, the first inhabitants of India were good-natured, peaceful, dark-skinned shepherds, called the Dravidians. They were supposedly remarkable builders, witness the city of Mohenjo-Daro in Pakistani Sind, but had no culture to speak-off, no written texts, no proper script even. Then, around 1500 B.C., India is said to have been invaded by tribes called the Aryans: white-skinned, nomadic people, who originated somewhere in Ural, or the Caucasus. To the Aryans, are attributed Sanskrit, the Vedic – or Hindu religion, India's greatest spiritual texts, the Vedas, as well as a host of subsequent writings, the Upanishads, the Mahabharata, the Ramanaya, etc...

This was indeed a masterly stroke on the part of the British : thanks to the Aryan theory, they showed on the one hand that Indian civilisation was not that ancient and that it was posterior to the cultures which influenced the western world – Mesopotamia, Sumeria, or Babylon – and on the other hand, that whatever good things India had developed – Sanskrit, literature, or even its architecture, had been influenced by the West. Thus, Sanskrit, instead of being the mother of all Indo-European languages, became just a branch of their huge family; thus, the religion of Zarathustra is said to have influenced Hinduism – as these Aryan tribes were believed to have transited through numerous countries, Persia being one, before reaching India - and not vice versa. In the same manner, many achievements were later attributed to the Greek invasion of Alexander the Great: scientific discoveries, mathematics, architecture etc. So ultimately, it was cleverly proved that nothing is Indian, nothing really great was created in India, it was always born out of different influences on the subcontinent.

To make this theory even more complicated, the British, who like other invaders before them had a tough time with the Brahmins and the Kshatriyas, implied that the Aryans drove the Dravidians southwards, where they are still today; and that to mark forever their social boundaries, these Aryans had devised the despicable caste system, whereby, they the priests and princes, ruled over the merchants and labourers... And thus English missionaries and later, American preachers, were able to convert tribes and low caste Hindus by telling them: "you, the aborigines, the tribals, the Harijans, were there in India before the Aryans; you are the *original* inhabitants of India, and you should discard Hinduism, the religion of these arrogant Aryans and embrace, Christianity, the true religion."

Thus, was born the great Aryan invasion theory, of two civilisations, that of the low caste Dravidians and the high caste Aryans, always pitted against each other – which has endured, as it is still today being used by some Indian politicians – and has been enshrined in all history books – Western, and unfortunately also Indian. Thus, were born wrong "nationalistic" movements, such as the Dravidian movement against Hindi and the much-maligned Brahmins, (see previous chapter) who actually represent today a minority, which is often underprivileged.... This Aryan invasion theory has also made India look westwards, instead of taking pride in its past and present achievements. It may also unconsciously be one of the reasons why there was at one time such great fascination for Sonia Gandhi, a White-Skinned-Westerner, who may have been unconsciously perceived as a true Aryan by the downtrodden Dravidians and a certain fringe of that Indian intelligentsia which is permanently affected by an inferiority complex towards the West. It may even have given a colour fixation to this country, where women will go to extremes to look "fair".

But today, this theory is being challenged more and more by new discoveries, both archaeological and linguistic. There are many such proofs: the discovery of the Saraswati river, the deciphering of the Indus seals and recent genetic discoveries. In the Rig Veda, the Ganges, India's sacred river, is only mentioned once, but the mythic Saraswati is praised on more than *fifty* occasions. Yet for a long time, the Saraswati river was considered a myth, until the American satellite Landstat was able to photograph and map the bed of this magnificent river, which was nearly fourteen kilometres wide, took its source in the Himalayas, flowed through the states of Haryana, Punjab and Rajasthan, before throwing itself in the sea near Bhrigukuccha, today called Broach. American archaeologist Mark Kenoyer was able to prove in 1991 that the majority of archaeological sites of the so-called Harappan (or Dravidian) civilisation were not situated on the ancient bed of the Indus river, as first thought, but on the Saraswati. Another archaeologist, Paul-Henri Francfort, Chief of a franco-american mission (Weiss, Courty, Weterstromm, Guichard,

Senior, Meadow, Curnow), which studied the Saraswati region at the beginning of the nineties, found out why the Saraswati had 'disappeared': « around 2200 B.C., he writes, an immense drought reduced the whole region to aridity and famine » (Evidence for Harappan irrigation system in Haryana and Rajasthan – Eastern Anthropologist 1992). Thus around this date, most inhabitants moved away from the Saraswati to settle on the banks of the Indus and Sutlej rivers.

According to official history, the Vedas were composed around 1500 BC, some even say 1200 BC. Yet, as we have seen, the Rig Veda, describes India as it was *before* the great drought which dried-up the Saraswati; which means in effect that the so-called Indus, or Harappan civilisation was a *continuation* of the Vedic epoch, which ended approximately when the Saraswati dried-up. Recently, the famous Indus seals, discovered on the site of Mohenja Daro and Harappa, may have been deciphered by Dr Rajaram, a mathematician who worked at one time for the NASA and Dr Jha, a distinguished linguist. In the biased light of the Aryan invasion theory, these seals were presumed to be written in a Harappan (read Dravidian) script, although they had never been convincingly decoded. But Rajaram and Jha, using an ancient Vedic glossary, the Nighantu, found out that the script is of Sanskrit lineage, is read from left to right and does not use vowels (which like in Arabic, are 'guessed' according to the meaning of the whole sentence). In this way, they have been able to decipher so far 1500 and 2000 seals, or about half the known corpus. As the discovery of the Saraswati river, the decipherment of the Indus scripts also goes to prove that that the Harappan Civilization, of which the seals are a product, belonged to the latter part of the Vedic Age and had close connections with Vedantic works like the Sutras and the Upanishads.

In this light, it becomes evident that not only there never was an Aryan invasion of India, but, as historian Konraad Elst writes, it could very well be that it was an Indian race which went westwards: "rather than Indo-Iranians on their way from South Russia to Iran and partly to India, these may as well be the Hitites, Kassites or Mitanni, on their way from *India*, via the Aral Lake area, to Anatolia, or Mesopotamia, where they show up in subsequent centuries" (Indigenous Indians).

The most recent discoveries are even more convincing as they deal with genes. A team comprised of scientists from Harvard Medical School, Broad Institute of Harvard and MIT, Birbal Sahni Institute of Palaeosciences, Lucknow, Centre for Cellular and Molecular Biology under the CSIR (Hyderabad), Max Planck Institute, Leipzig, Germany and University of California, USA and Deccan College Post Graduate and Research Institute, Pune, researched on DNA samples collected from a 4,500-year-old female skeleton excavated from a Harappan site in Rakhigarhi, Haryana. The research demonstrated that there was no trace of any foreign genetic presence in them « which proves that people belonging to the Indus Valley Civilization had distinct genetic lineage," emphasized Prof Thangaraj of CCMB, Hyderabad.

Prof Vasant Shinde, director, Deccan College further stated: « we discovered that there was no detectable ancestry from Steppe pastoralists or from Anatolian and Iranian farmers, suggesting farming in South Asia arose from local foragers rather than from large-scale migration from the West »...

There goes the famous Aryan's invasion theory from which even staunch defenders like Romila Thapar, have even taken a distance.

CHAPTER 22

Ayodhya: Hinduphobia at its Peak

The Ayodhya case was heard in 2019 by a Constitution Bench of Chief Justice of India Ranjan Gogoi and Justices SA Bobde, DY Chandrachud, Ashok Bhushan and Abdul Nazeer, this followed the failed mediation between Hindus and Muslims by Sri Sri Ravi Shankar, Sriram Panchu and Mister Kallifulla, a retired supreme court judge. After arguments on behalf of the Hindu parties to the Ayodhya dispute concluded, arguments commenced on behalf of the Muslim parties to the case. Later, rejoinder arguments on behalf of the Hindu deity Ram Lalla were also being made.

In the Babri Masjid demolition case, it is necessary to against cast a look towards this path-breaking event, that signalled the waking-up of Hindus and that for the first time in centuries, they would not take anymore things lying down. How many of those judges who have lambasted the "Hindu fundamentalists" and lamented the destruction of the Babri Masjid mosque as the "death of secularism in India", have been to Ayodhya? (not Faizabad, mind you, which is Ayodhya's twin Muslim city). When one arrived in Ayodhya before the destruction of the mosque, one was struck by the fact that it was a Hindu town "par excellence". More than Benares even, it is dotted everywhere with innumerable temples; it has all these old Hindus houses and this lovely river with its ghats which runs through the lower town. And then, forlorn on the top, there was this lone mosque with its two ugly domes, which looked so out of place and unused, that anyone with a right sense -and that includes the Muslims- should see that it was not worth making an issue of.

The destruction of the Babri Masjid has evoked – and is still evoking today – such fiery reactions, that the importance of Ayodhya has been totally overlooked: Ayodhya is a *symbol,* through which two India's are facing each other. And the outcome of their confrontation will shape the future of this country for generations to come.

The first India wants to be secular and unite together through an egalitarian, democratic spirit all the minorities, ethnic groups, religions and people of the country.

But the question is: what would be the binding element of this kind of India? Secularism, says the first side. But secularism has a different meaning for each one, as we saw in the preceding chapters. For the British, it was a convenient way to divide and rule, by treating each Indian community on par, although some were in minority and others in majority, thereby planting the seeds of separatisms. For the Congress Party, it has always meant giving in to the Muslims' demands, because its leaders never could really make out if the allegiance of Indian Muslims first want to India and then to Islam – or vice-versa. And for India's intelligentsia, its writers, journalists, top bureaucrats, the majority of whom are Hindus, it means, apart from spitting on its own religion and brothers, an India which would be a faithful copy of the West: liberal, modern, atheist, industrialised, intellectual and western-oriented.

Furthermore, what makes India unique? Certainly not its small elite which apes the West. Nor its modern youth, whom you meet in Delhi's swank parties. Not even its political, bureaucratic and judicial system; it's a copy of the British set up, which is not fully adapted to India's unique character and conditions. What then?

The second India which is confronting the other at Ayodhya is of a course the India of the Hindus. When Imam Bhukari and others state that "we (the Mughals) gave everything to this country, its culture, its manners, its arts (and he adds: "the Hindus by destroying the Babri Masjid show how little gratitude they have"), apart from making a pompous declaration, he proclaims exactly the opposite of the reality. Because the truth is that not only Hinduism is what makes India unique, so different from all the other nations of the world, but it is the single most important influence in Indian history. In the words of Sri Aurobindo: "The inner principle of Hinduism, the most tolerant and receptive of all religious systems, is not sharply exclusive like the religious spirit of Christianity or Islam ... it is the fulfilment of the highest tendencies of human civilisation and it will include in its sweep the most vital impulses of modern life."

And indeed, if you look at India today, you find that Hinduism has permeated, influenced, shaped, every part of this country, every religion, every culture. Be it the Christians who are like no other Catholics of the world, or Indian Muslims, who whatever they may say, are utterly different from their brothers in Saudi Arabia. But Hinduism is too narrow a word, it's a corruption of the original word "Indu", for true Hinduism is Dharma, India's infinite and eternal spiritual knowledge, which took shape into so many varied expressions throughout the ages, be it the Vedantas, Buddhism, or the Arya Samaj and which is today still very much alive in India, particularly in its rural masses, which after all constitute 80% of its population.

What one has to grasp is that Ayodhya only makes sense when the immense harm the Muslims did to India is not **negated**, as indeed it has been and still is today, whether in Kashmir, where the last Hindus were made to flee in terror, or in Bangladesh, where the crowds still regularly go on rampage against Hindus and their temples (as told by a Bangladeshi Muslim herself, Talisma Nasreen). It is in this light, that it becomes extraordinary for an impartial observer to see today that when *for once*, the Hindus wanted to displace, not even to destroy, one mosque and rebuild the "temple", which they believe was built in this particular place, for one of their most cherished Gods, the one which is loved universally by all, men, women, children, they are treated as rabid fundamentalists. The great Mughals must be laughing all the way down their graves! What a reversal of situation! What a turnabout of history! And when the mosque was destroyed, it evoked such fiery reactions, such pompous, overblown, sanctimonious, holier-than-thou, atrocious, ridiculous, sly and totally undeserved outrage, both within India and in the Western world (who should be the last one to give lessons to India), that the importance of Ayodhya as a symbol has been totally overlooked.

The obvious trap is to think that the demolition of the mosque in Ayodhya is something to gloat about and that it is the duty of all good Hindus to see that other important mosques at Mathura, Vanarasi, or elsewhere, be also razed to the ground; or that all cities with a Muslim name be renamed with a Hindu one. This is not true Hinduism, which has always shown its tolerance and accepted in its fold other creeds and faiths. Indeed a true "Indu" India will be secular in the correct sense of the term: it will give freedom to each religion, each culture, so that it develops itself in the bosom of a Greater India, of which dharma, true spirituality, will be the cementing factor.

Nevertheless, the destruction of the Babri Masjid, however unfortunate, has made its point: the occult Mughal hold over Hindu India has been broken and centuries of Hindu submission erased. Hindus have proved that they too can fight. The time of Hindu power has indeed come

Muslim respondents in the Ayodhya case were claiming in November 2019 that there is no justification for the title in Ayodhya by Hindus until 1989 and required the restoration of Babri Masjid as it stood before demolition in 1992. What rubbish! When Muslims built this mosque on one of the most sacred Hindu temples ever!

Luckily, on 9 November 2019, the Supreme Court cleared the way for the construction of the Ram Mandir on the 2.77 acre disputed site and allotted 5 acres of land in the Ayodhya vicinity for the Muslims to build a mosque. Victory for the Hindus. But at what cost?

CHAPTER 23

Negationism of Hindu Genocide

Belgium Indologist, Koenraad Elst, defined very well what is Negationism: 'Negate truth, as many times as possible, even if it is outrageous, until it puts doubt in people's minds.'

Hitler's propaganda Minister, Goebbels, was the first one to use Negationism on a large scale and since then, it has been utilized by many historians, to negate for instance the Holocaust of 6 million Jews by Hitler, which was so well documented (I have good German friends in Auroville, who tell me '6 millions, impossible'!), and in India, to negate the genocide of Muslim invasions and replace it, as Romila Thapar has done, 'that it was only because there was so much gold in Hindu temples and thus it was not a religious crusade.'

In my humble opinion, the Congress has used skilfully and efficiently Negationism in cases of the Rafale and the Balakot strike in 2019. Most of us, when Mr. Modi announced the Rafale deal in Paris, thought it was a brilliant stroke, absolutely above board, but after so many stories, counter stories, denials, counter-denials, doubt crept in the minds of many and the Congress certainly has gained a few points. The same is true of the 2019 strike against the Kashmiri terrorists training camp in Balakot, Pakistan: it appeared to me that much of the glow and national pride that rose immediately after the strike, has diffused, and people gave some credibility to an often hostile western and even Indian media and their satellite photos.

Instead of keeping a dignified 'above the fray' attitude and have some of its spokespersons, speak for instance about Negationism, citing examples, the BJP Govt allowed itself to descend into arguments and counter-arguments and hence gave some grip to the lies and untruth of the Media, the Congress and Rahul Gandhi, which are asuric in nature and anti-dharmic.

Once more, the PM may need some out of the box advice from non-BJP, non-Government friends and well-wishers, who have experience. It is essential that he incarnates true Hindu power, so as to implement crucial reforms in the fields of the Constitution Education, the Judiciary, etc, without which India cannot fulfil the dreams of Swami Vivekananda, Sri Aurobindo and so many avatars. At the moment though, it looks to me and quite a few others, that he does not want to be seen as incarnating Hindu power. Yet was he not elected by 97% Hindus- the remaining 3% only, by minorities? Hindu power needs to fight Negationism at all costs. We see how it is used to paralyse the Parliament, to belittle Hindus and their beliefs. And however, much Narendra Modi tries to be 'secular', he and his party, the BJP, will continue to be attacked with false claims, accusations of attacks on minorities, fascism, etc. This is true Negationism and it aims to destroy Hindu power.

Hinduism has been one of the most peaceful creeds in the world, accepting the reality of different beliefs, never trying to convert – even in a non-violent manner, like the Buddhists did in Asia – and submitting itself rather meekly, except for a Shivaji, a Guru Gobind or a Rani of Jhansi, to numerous invasions. The same thing cannot be said about Islam, whatever N. Ram says in Frontline. Many historians, amongst them Will Durant, Louis Frederick, or Alain Danielou, have remarked that the Muslim invaders were so certain that they were doing their holy duty by razing temples and killing Hindus, that they had recorded down carefully and proudly their deeds in their own archives.

Mahmud of Ghazni, for instance, who patronized art and literature, would recite a verse of the Koran every night after having razed temples and killed his quota of unbelievers. Firuz Shah Tughlak, personally confirms that the destruction of Pagan temples was done out of piety and writes: "on the day of a Hindu festival, I went there myself, ordered the executions of all the leaders and practionners of his abomination; I destroyed their idols temples and built mosques in their places." Aurangzeb did not just build an isolated mosque on a razed temple, as Romila Thapar would like us to believe, he ordered all temples destroyed, among them the Kashi Vishvanath, one of the most sacred places of Hinduism and had mosques built on a number of cleared temples sites. All other Hindu sacred places within his reach equally suffered destruction, with mosques built on them. A few examples: Krishna's birth temple in Mathura, the rebuilt Somnath temple on the coast of Gujurat, the Vishnu temple replaced with the Alamgir mosque now overlooking Benares and the Treta-ka-Thakur temple in Ayodhya. The number of temples destroyed by Aurangzeb is counted in 4, if not 5 figures. This is a small excerpt of his own official court chronicles: "Aurangzeb ordered all provincial governors to destroy all schools and temples of the Pagans and to make a complete end to all pagan teachings and practices." Or: "Hasan Ali Khan came and said that 172 temples in the area had been destroyed.... His majesty went to Chittor and 63 temples were destroyed. Abu Tarab, appointed to destroy the idol-temples of Amber, reported that 66 temples had been razed to the ground». Aurangzeb did not stop at destroying temples, their users were also wiped-out; even his own brother, Dara Shikoh, was executed for taking an interest in Hindu religion and the Sikh Guru Tegh Bahadur was beheaded because he objected to Aurangzeb's forced conversions. As we can see Romila Thapar and Percival Spear's statement of a benevolent Aurangzeb is a flagrant attempt at negationism (the negation of historical crimes). Even the respectable Encyclopedia Britannica in its entry on India, does not mention in its chapter on the Sultanate period any persecutions of Hindus by Muslims, except "that Firuz Shah Tughlaq made largely unsuccessful attempts at converting his Hindu subjects and sometime persecuted them."

Indian school books seem to have taken their cue from the Encyclopedia Britannica, as there is hardly any mention of this dark aspect of India's past. But why does India negate its history? We know that Nehru and Gandhi wanted to keep Pakistan within India and wished to avoid the splintering away of Muslim groups. But was it a good enough reason to suppress information about Muslim atrocities during ten centuries of bloody invasions and the massive destruction of Hindu temples? On the contrary this has only created more terrorism. Denying and suppressing the history cannot keep the harmony. In its place, truth and reconciliation are necessary. Hiding the truth denies sympathy to the victim, civilization and culture. A nation unless, it is ready to face its own history – the Good and the Bad, the Courageous and the Cowardly – can never bloom into its full plenitude. Hidden aspects of its own history sooner or later will surface and bring with them the guilt, anger, regret, which are the necessary ingredients to wipe-off that particular black karma. In Germany, for instance, Germans have been reminded again and again about the atrocities committed by the Nazis during World War II, and that has brought a sense of guilt, which has acted as a deterrent to future atrocities The Jews have constantly tried, since the Nazi genocide, to keep alive the remembrance of their six million martyrs. This has got nothing to do with vengeance. Do the Jews of today want to retaliate upon contemporary Germany? No. It is only a matter of making sure that history does not repeat its mistakes, as alas it is doing today in India: witness the persecution of Hindus in Kashmir, whose 350,000 Pandits have fled their 5000-year-old homeland, or the oppression of Hindus in Bangladesh and Pakistan. To remember, is to be able to look at today with the wisdom of yesterday. No collective memory should be erased for appeasing a particular community. Hiding the facts and justifying past Muslim crimes has led to terrorism in the Indian sub-continent. Muslims were never held accountable. One of the first steps to curb violence is to make one aware of past mistakes. Guilt in the culprit and forgiveness in the victim can put an end to self-righteousness and the kind of terrorism we see today in Kashmir, with the support of Pakistan.

CHAPTER 24

The Karma of being a Muslim

The International Media keeps asking this important question: are Muslims today unfairly targeted? Are they subjected to needless harassment? What started at US airports (Muslims, such as actor Shah Rukh Khan questioned) could soon extend to railway stations, borders, shopping malls, even... One day, it could very well be that anybody who looks like a Muslim will be regarded suspiciously in the streets.

At first glance it looks really unjust. Yet, if we observe closely the events in the past twenty years, we see that not only the Muslim community has never cared to collectively condemn the atrocities which are committed all around the world by Muslim terrorists, but that many of them condone it in the name of Kashmir, Palestine or Chechnya. If you take the most recent attacks in India, such as the 26/11 Mumbai ones, for instance, you find that Javed Akhtar, a Muslim, does write a poetic tearjerker ("As a human being, I shudder to think how can my fellow humans do something so heinous? Are these terrorists made of flesh and blood? Do they laugh and cry like us"?). But not once Akhtar, who has made a favorite pastime of deriding Hindu Gurus, said that all these crimes are committed in the name of Islam and the Koran, "his" religion and "his" Scriptures...

Yes, we do occasionally come across wonderful Muslims, open, friendly, who have somehow preserved the knowledge that all religions are the same, that Islam in India owes a lot to the tolerance of Indians, that Hinduism, yoga, meditation and pranayama, are India's gifts to the world and can be practiced by Muslims, Christians and Hindus alike. I have personally met quite a few of them, within the

Art of Living Family, for example. But they are such rarities. And even those educated Muslims, whom you can talk to, will not go as far as criticizing the Koran.

So will Islam ultimately convert itself? Because the problem is not with Muslims, but with the Koran. This is why it appears so unfair that innocent, peace loving Muslims are targeted today by security forces. But it has always been the law of Karma that a nation or a community collectively pays for the deeds of its own members. Will then Islam, instead of feeling totally paranoiac, thinking that it is under attack everywhere, whether it is Palestine, Chechnya, Kashmir, or France, realize that it is actually *Islam which is the aggressor* all over the world, that Muslims who have settled in France or India, or the UK, and which these countries have *sincerely* accepted, giving them citizenship and the same rights as any French, Indian or German citizens, are actually biting the hand that fed them ? Will the mullahs of Islam accept to sit down and reform the Koran, which is a perfectly acceptable scripture for the Middle ages, when mentalities were very different, but which today still propagates an aggressive, exclusive, and dangerous zeal in its children?

This is what we are all hoping for. This is what most Western leaders secretly crave for, when they go out of their way to praise and favour the moderate Muslims of their country. This is what spiritual leaders like His Holiness Sri Sri Ravi Shankar are attempting, with a certain amount of success, by speaking to Muslim leaders, fostering ties in Muslim countries such as Iraq or Afghanistan, or reforming Kashmiri terrorists through meditation.

Unfortunately, time is running out. Muslims in India and elsewhere in the world do not understand is that *we are slowly losing our innocence*. At the moment, Islam still benefits from the sympathy of the media, which constantly negates Islamic fundamentalism, making a hero for instance of the Chechen warlord Shamil Bassayev, killed a few years ago, who organized the gruesome massacre of hundreds of children in Beslan – and a villain of Vladimir Putin (or a hero of Kashmiri militants and a monster of Modi) but it is slowly losing that sympathy. Sooner or later nearly the entire world will wage a war against Islam, from Europe to China, from the Ural to Pakistan.

There will also come a time, which is not very far, as recent incidents have shown, where everybody will become wary of anything Islamic. Anyone looking slightly Muslim, in a plane, in a train, in a shopping mall, will be looked upon suspiciously. Anybody with a Muslim name will have problems entering any country. Those who have Muslim friends will quietly stop seeing them or find some excuses not to meet them. It is already happening. Muslims will cry themselves hoarse and speak of persecution. But they will have only themselves to blame: they did not speak up as a community when innocents all over the world were killed in the name of their religion.

And this may be the way Islam might slowly disappear. Muslims with a little common sense, or just maybe with a sense of survival, will start changing their names quietly, they will stop going to the Mosque, they will send their children to Christian or Hindu schools. Governments will clamp down so hard on their own Muslims, there will be so many restrictions on them, that entire families, will move out of the Muslim enclaves you find all over the world, to resettle elsewhere. Jehadis facing certain death even if they are not suicide bombers, will melt back in civilian life. Muslims will slowly lose faith in the righteousness and the power of their own religion, become atheists, or even embrace back Hinduism, as 90% of Muslims in India are Hindu converts. It may take a few decades, a hundred years even, But Islam will surely disappear in the alleys of history and what now appears like a menacing, dangerous, foreboding force, will be looked upon as just another religion that came and passed away.

Unless Islam converts itself...

CHAPTER 25

Islam and the Bhagavad Gita

Often, I have been often branded as an Islamophobe or a hard-line pro-Hindu, because I have also advocated the coming of age of Hindu Power after 450 years of decline and slumber....

As I said before, I started seeing the light when I began covering Kashmir during the 90s, after separatism bloomed and violence set fire to the Valley. It is there that I witnessed the first Hindu leaders whom I had interviewed previously, assassinated in the most savage manner, such as doctors, lawyers, or All India radio broadcasters. And then, when Benazir Bhutto gave her famous speech of 'Azad Kashmir', every mosque in Srinagar and the Valley repeated that cry, telling Hindus: "Convert or die". And in a few weeks, 350,000 Kashmiri Pandits left their ancestral houses and land, for no other crime than being Hindus – and that without firing a shot in self-defence – becoming refugees in their own country, a first in the world.

Since then, covering many other countries, I witnessed the same phenomenon in Bangladesh, Pakistan or Afghanistan, of Hindus being the target of hatred, as Jews have been for centuries. This set me to study Indian history and I quickly realised that great Hindu heroes (see previous chapter) such as Shivaji Maharaj or Maharana Pratap, had been bypassed in Indian history books, to a single paragraph: Shivaji Maharaj who represent one of the best instances of true Hindu Power and fought alone with his wits, extraordinary courage and a few hundred men, defeated the most powerful army of the world of his time, is a 'plunderer'; and Maharana Pratap, also an incarnation of wonderful, secular, fearless Hindu Power, is described as a small chieftain, although he is the only Rajput to have fought the Moghols and to have held Akbar's army at bay the Hadilghati battle. The irony is that tyrants such as Aurangzeb, who were monsters not only towards Hindus but also with their own family – Aurangzeb poisoned his own father, beheaded his brother Dara Shikoh, imprisoned his son – are lauded in history books as 'firm but just emperors under whom arts flourished' (Aurangzeb actually banned music at his court, because it was un-Islamic)....

... It happens that my wife and myself are teachers of the pranayama and meditation techniques of Sri Sri Ravi Shankar, which we have practicing for the last 25 years and which have changed our lives, giving us energy, enthusiasm and commitment. We do this free, as a sewa, to partake of this great gift to humanity that originates from India.

We taught once in Sri Sri's Bangalore ashram a pranayama course to a batch of Iranians. Our group, which had many girls and ladies, some of them who always covered their heads, was reserved at first, but as the course progressed, there grew a bond of affection and warmth between us all. We could perceive so much love and humanity in all of them. And by the end of the course, we all danced and hugged each other.

Now it is not because I have fought Islam and strove for Hindu Power, that I did no know before this course that Muslims are as much as the others, decent human beings, warm, family oriented, hospitable. I remember when I drove to India by road from Paris, crossing many Muslim countries. My best friend was then a Muslim French Moroccan. He would say *"Assalam-o-Alaikum »,* and doors would open, smiles were flashed, we would be dined, entertained, respected. This universal brotherhood of Islam does not exist in the Hindu world.

So this set me thinking: Islam was born in Iran and since Khomeini's takeover, though it has a Shia majority, Iran has an image of a hard-core Islamic nation, where the Sharia reigns supreme and which is ready even to use a nuclear weapon to impose the supremacy of its faith. Yet these people we taught were the opposite and showed values of refinement and love that are today missing in the western Christian world....

I do understand even more now that most Muslims are good, witness the many human right organizations, journalists or intellectuals that fight for their rights as refugees, at the moment Yet the stumbling block remains *the Koran*, a wonderful scripture, no doubt, but which was written for people and mentalities of 1400 years ago, when realities were harsh, punishments even harsher and survival a matter of life and death. Nobody has read the Koran properly, except the Islamic terrorists of today: it does say that the Infidels should be slayed, that Islam must be the world religion, that women can be stoned if unfaithful, or that being gay is a crime punishable by death. Logic would say that Muslim scholars of international repute should get together and reform the Koran, as Christians have done, so that it becomes adapted to the 21st century world. Problem is that nobody dares touch it or question it for fear of death. Problem is that even within the most moderate, educated and enlightened Muslims, logic and good sense, stops when it comes to the Koran....

Thus, I will continue fighting Islam, in the sprit of the Bhagavad Gita: so many of my brothers and sisters are in the opposite camp. I have come to love them and respect them too.... Yet, I know that willingly or unwillingly, consciously or unconsciously, by accident or by karma, they are born in a religion that is harming the world, that is on the side of the anti-human and anti-divine forces. Therefore, it must be challenged by Hindu Power, even if it is with love in the heart – and not hatred.

CHAPTER 26

How to Counter Hinduphobia?

The BJP has the habit of either keeping quiet under attack, or of overreacting with statements that are immediately seized upon by the Media and termed as intolerant, saffron, right wing etc. Yet, if the MP's, MLA's, spokespersons were groomed in workshops to speak in a cold, logical, statistical manner, their arguments could not be refuted and would not evoke these 'intolerant', OR 'saffron' accusations. Here is a sample of what the BJP MP's, MLA's, spokespersons, could be groomed into.

BEEF. When questioned about the ban on beef in certain states, instead of being on the defensive or quoting some vague Vedic scriptures, use environmental arguments, which today are politically correct. For instance, tell your detractors that cows must consume 16 kilos of vegetation in order to convert them into 1 kilo of meat. Raising beef for food consumes more than half of all water used in the U.S. It takes 2,500 litres of water to produce a kilo of beef but only 25 liters to produce a kilo of wheat. Producing just one beefsteak uses enough fossil fuel to drive a small car 32 kilometres. Of all raw materials and fossil fuels used in the U.S., more than one-third is devoted to raising animals for food.

MINORITIES. When the Opposition or the Media says that minorities are persecuted in India, remind them that the first Christian community, that of the Syrians, settled in Kerala in the first century and have practiced their faith freely ever since; or that the Jews came to India, mostly in Cochin and Mumbai in the 6th century, after the sack of the temple of Jerusalem and that India is the ONLY country in the world where Jews were NEVER persecuted; talk also about the Parsis, who were welcomed in India after they fled Iran under Muslim persecution, and integrated beautifully in this country, producing stalwarts, such as JRD Tata; you can finish by saying that today Tibetan culture is mostly defunct at the hand of the Chinese in Tibet – but very much alive in India (Dharamsala), where the Dalai Lama and his followers were given refuge.

INTOLERANCE. When accusations of intolerance are thrown at you, just remind your interlocutor that a Hindu, still today, recognizes the fact that God manifests Himself or Herself at different times, under different names, using different scriptures. This concept allows Hindus from the villagers to the upper castes, to enter a church or even a Mosque with respect and devotion. Indeed, today Hindus still go to Darghas, such as one in Ajmer, and worship there. Point out to your detractors that the reverse is not true and that a Muslim or even an Indian Christian, may think that they are committing a sin by entering in a Hindu temple.

RSS. One of the most common ploys of anti-Hindu intellectuals is to always equate the RSS with the Taliban or the ISIS. Instead of being flustered, ask your accusers to provide you statistics – of say the last ten years – of how many innocent people the ISIS, the Taliban, the Lakshar-e-Taiba and others have been killed – and how many the RSS and various Hindu groups have. You will see that they will come-up with no numbers for the RSS, as even the Malegaon train blast have not been proved. You can also add the RSS is mostly a group of old fuddy daddies with their funny kaki shorts (trousers are coming now, smile at them!) and lathi sticks, and that most of them who would not harm a fly.

CASTES and DALITS. When pounced upon about Dalits being persecuted under the BJP rule, like a few years back after the suicide of Rohit Vemula in Hyderabad, point out that even though there are still intolerable castes abuses, mostly in deep rural areas such as UP or Bihar, and mostly between low castes (often between converted Dalits or Tribals and non-converted ones-. Highlight the fact that throughout Indian history Dalits have risen to the highest levels.

Valmiki – composer of Mahabharata, which also contains the Bhagavad Gita, was a fisherman (initially a highway robber). The composer of the Ramayana. Maharshi Ved Vyas, was too the son of a fisherwoman. Chandragupta Maurya and the Maurya Dyanasty, were all from the Muria tribe which used to collect Peacock (Mor) feathers. Queen Ahiliabai of Indore (see chapter above), one of the most enlightened rulers of Middle Ages India (she had an army of women), was adopted from a lower class by the king....

Say also that today there are many dalit chief ministers, such as Mayavati, or Presidents of India (Kocheril Raman Narayanan) and one of India's most revered saints, Amrita Anandamayi, comes from the lowest caste possible, that of the fishermen of Kerala. Yet, she is worshiped by millions of Indians, many of them from upper castes who prostrate themselves at her feet. Many of the brilliant minds in the west, professors, doctors, scientists, have helped her, build the most modern hospitals in India, or top class universities, such as one in Coimbatore. 'see below a more complete list of famous dalits)

BHARAT MATA KI JAI. When intellectuals or the Media object to the chanting of *Bharat Mata ki* Jai or *Vande Mataram*, just quietly point out that the West has no qualms about being a Christian civilization. Barack Obama (or Donald Trump), for instance, though, partly of African Muslim origin, swore twice on the Bible to become President of the United States. Many European countries have deep Christian roots and schools offer compulsory classes on the Bible, France although a secular state, has 80% Catholics who attend mass and put their children in Christian schools. Yet, we see in India, a country with 80% Hindu majority, where freedom of worship has always been the rule, that anything Hindu is frowned upon. This is totally wrong and it is a leftover of three centuries of British colonization. Point out, that Hinduism is the only religion in the world that never used its armies, like Islam and Christianity did, to convert others. It never even sent missionaries like the Buddhists, but instead Hinduism peacefully spread abroad, to the East, witness the grandeur of Angkor Vat, or the West, where yoga and meditation, Hindu practices, are today prevalent.

MAHATMA GANDHI. One of the most common attacks against Hindus is to say that a Hindu fanatic, a RSS one, killed the great Mahatma Gandhi. If you want to throw your attacker off, just nod and say 'yes, I agree – and I condemn it'. This will close the conversation. You can l also point out that he was judged and hanged. No need to go into the harm that Gandhi did to the nation by always pandering to the Muslim fanatic voices.

GURUS. Since the Independence, the Indian Media has been regularly attacking Gurus from Osho, Sai Baba, or even today Sri Sri Ravi Shankar, as it happened recently during the Word Cultural Festival of March 2016. Point out skilfully that guru-ship is a very ancient Indian tradition, that even pervades in the arts. Dancers for instance, have teachers that they revere as gurus, touching their feet or bowing down to them before starting their practice. Even great Muslim musicians have adopted and accepted this tradition. Instead of going after gurus, tell your confronters, they should target the millions of disciples that these masters have all over the world. The combined number of disciples of the great gurus alive today must be reaching a hundred million. If the Media or the intellectuals had any courage and common sense they would go after these – which they can't, so that will silence them....

APEX BODY FOR SCHOOLS OF JOURNALISM

No doubt, censorship is *not* the answer to the Indian Media's hostility both towards the BJP and India's ancient spirituality, plus the fact that Modi's governance, since he has become PM, has already made himself quite popular in his own right. Yet, Media houses like NDTV or TOI, which have been traditionally pro-Congress and anti-Hindu, can be indirectly taken to task, without the PM appearing to be involved – the former because there is a 100 crore scam more quite well documented against it – the latter as it has been caught many times doing paid news.

But the real problem lies in Indian schools of journalism, which are deeply entrenched in a Marxist thought and keep churning out young journalists in the same mould. The solution would be for the Government *to create an apex body that would chart a single curriculum as well as guidelines for schools of journalism* which would teach a bit of true Indian History, a bit of yoga and pranayama, pride of motherland, along with the latest techniques in electronic and web journalism. I personally can be involved in that venture

Institute of Indology

One of the reasons for India's wrong image abroad, which in turn results in lesser investments than say China, is that the western Indologists – Witzel, Donniger in the USA, Jaffrelot, Subramanyam, and others in France – keep harping on India's problems – castes, poverty, so called-Hindu fundamentalism, etc. I know for a fact that in France, it has an influence on the top bureaucrats and the politicians, as every time something important happens in India – elections, catastrophes, riots, etc, their slanted opinions are sought by newspapers radios and televisions. In France, even after Modi has been elected and has shown vision in his statesmanship, the Media has remained fairly hostile, French investment in India has not increased and neither the French President nor his External Affairs Minister have taken much notice of India. It is true, as Modi has proved in America, that given time, they will have to acknowledge India's rise, but why not speed up the process? *The idea is to hunt for more friendly Indologists, which are there, but are shunted by the existing ones*, and promote them by inviting them to India and give them material which they can use in their own countries. We can start by the USA, UK, France and Germany.

Thus it is proposed to set up an Institute of Indology endowed with clearly defined and distinctive goals, a specific identity, an efficient functioning and rich outputs and with genuine researched in Indology and 'Hindulogy' a new word that should be coined.

A Museum of Hindu Power (see next chapter)

We see more and more today that Indian History has to be rewritten according to the latest linguistic and archaeological discoveries, if

Indian children are to understand who they are and where they come from. We know now that not only the history of India's beginnings were written by European colonizers, with an intention to downsize, downgrade and postdate Indian civilization, but that unfortunately, generation after generation of Marxist Indian historians, for their own selfish purposes, endorsed and perpetuated these wrong theories, such as the Aryan invasion, which divided India like nothing else, pitting South against North, Aryan against Dravidian, Untouchables against Brahmins.

Hence the need for a Museum of Indian History, where the real Indian History will be engraved in stone and artefacts for generation to come.

CHAPTER 27

A Museum of Hindu Power

I had just completed my 18th year and I was living in Paris, France, the city of my birth, when I heard that a caravan of cars was driving from Paris to Pondicherry. I had never heard of India, but something in me pushed me to go. Thus in approx. 6 weeks, we crossed ten countries and had many adventures. We reached Delhi, driving from Lahore, in late September 1969.

I spent my first night in India in the Sri Aurobindo ashram New Delhi, in Aurobindo marg. As I said, I knew nothing about India and had no interest in spirituality. In those days, there were still fields in this part of Delhi. It was evening by the time we settled. I had with me a book of Sri Aurobindo, called the Life Divine, which I had never managed to read. I climbed on one of the vans with which we had come. It was a very beautiful sunset as you often see in India. I felt so peaceful: birds were singing, farmers were coming home. I opened the book and read a few lines. Suddenly I had a strong spiritual experience, a feeling of intense peace and joy and in a few seconds an intuition of what was karma, reincarnation, and of the worlds that were opening to me. Also, an immediate knowledge that I would live in India for the rest of my life.

This is believe, was an experience of Mother India. As many saints have said, India is not just a piece of land, it is the living Shakti, a body that, in spite of so many assaults over the centuries, as our Hindu Tolerance exhibition has shown, still radiates knowledge and power to whomsoever opens to it. My first guru was Mother India and to Her I dedicate this shrine and our Museum.

Of course, 2 weeks later in Pondicherry I met the Mother, Sri Aurobindo's companion - and it was the turning point of my life: my whole outlook turned upside down – or rather, became as it should be. Since then, it is my strong belief that Mother India guided me in all these years: often, for instance, I have felt spontaneously 'at home' in some cities in India, as if I knew them from before. Places like Almora in the Himalayas, for instance, where we have had powerful intuitions on how ancient our souls are.

I even had this experience in Srinagar. I covered Kashmir as a journalist for the largest French political daily in the worst of its unrest, from the late eighties till the Kargil war. It is there without any doubt that I went through some of the most dangerous incidents of my life – and where I acquired, I think, a little bit of fearlessness, which has helped me till today. There was only one hotel opened for journalists during the unrest, it was called Adhoos and it was on the banks of the river Jhelum. There was curfew most of the time and nobody could go out without a pass, but at night I would step out of the hotel and walk on the bund that stops the river Jhelum from overflowing into Srinagar. One could hear gunfire and sometimes-even grenades in the distance, yet I could feel the presence of the millions of saints, yogis, avatars and simple people who had prayed and meditated for thousands of years in Kashmir. It seems today like an abstract experience, but on the spot, it was so strong and vivid and I felt that this was the very reason that India should keep Kashmir, for its sacredness and the Mother's presence in spite of all the strife.

I came to Pune 12 years ago for an Art of Living course. In the same way I immediately felt at home here. The course happened in a beautiful Jain temple outside the city. I knew of course about Shivaji Maharaj, having researched him for my books and becoming a long-standing admirer of him. I had some time after the course and I asked my driver to take me to the main Museum, which is called Kelkar. I was surprised and shocked to find that there was not a single exhibit on Shivaji and that in the city of his birth, there was no Museum worth the name honoring him. Great men and women who walk this earth and are instruments of God, do most of their work while in their physical body. But when they die, I believe they leave something behind, a presence, a will, an influence. This day I felt that I should do something to honor Shivaji Maharaj who was so devoted to his country, which he worshipped as the Mother and the idea of a Museum of true Indian History, dedicated to Shivaji Maharaj, started taking shape in my mind. Pune is the ideal place for this Museum: it's Shivaji Maharaj's realm, it is central to India and easily accessible from the South or the North and more than anything, Marathas have a stronger national fiber than in other states and I felt the Museum will be better protected here.

Yet, having spent the first 18 years of my life France, I still believe in logic and understanding with the mind. What is then the purpose of the Shivaji Maharaj shrine and of the Museum? Firstly, this is a place of knowledge. People can come to the temple, meditate, pray to Mother India or do a puja and come down a bit from their heads to their hearts. Then, they can learn something about the history of their country in the three exhibition halls, while the main Museum comes-up. Programs can also happen in our small amphitheater: films made by our foundation FACT can be screened, plays, satsangs can happen, art of living courses. Some of the Pune youth can come out feeling a little prouder of being Indian, a little more knowledgeable about the history of this great civilization that is India. It is a tragedy that the Indian education system produces so many brilliant youth, who are just good for export, as they are not made to learn about their own history, poets, avatars, legends.

We would like to have many Bharat Mata temples such as ours in Pune, along with one exhibition hall, come up, first all over Maharashtra, then in Gujarat and eventually, if God wills, all over India. It can be dedicated to different heroes and heroins: In Maharashtra it could also be dedicated to Dr Ambedkar, who is a true son of Bombay; in Rajasthan it can be dedicated to Rana

Pratap, in Madhya Padesh Ahylyabai or Rani of Jhansi, in Karnataka Chennamai, in Tamil Nadu to poet Bharati, and so on.

This is a difficult project. Whoever has never attempted to raise money for a Museum should give it a try. I have met hundreds of potential donors, but when you say, "I need funds to build a Museum of Indian History, as it happened, not as it has been written," you can see the mind of your interlocutor doing click and then pat comes the answer: "oh I have to speak to my board, oh, we only give to for health or education projects," full stop. There must be a reason why there is no Museum of Shivaji Maharaj worth the name in Pune, for at every step we encountered problems, some foreseen, some unforeseen, some even coming from our own people. The Chief Minister of Maharashtra, Mr. Fadvanis, was so impressed by a presentation of the museum by my wife Namrita and myself in January 2019 that he gave a grant of 2 crores rupees. His bureaucrats sat on it – until today we have not receive the money! Trying to portray Indian History as it happened, not as it has been written, is a very sensitive task that leaves one exposed to all kind of troubles. We even are facing some threats from some Shivaji group, who objects to Shivaji Maharaj being associated with Mother India or the Vedas. Shivaji was an extraordinary being, an instrument of god and whoever binds him to a particular caste, or even a particular guru, demeans him and hampers his work, for he was a supra national figure and his qualities of dedication to Mother India, of extreme courage, of respect of human rights and honest administration, are badly needed in today's India.

This is just a humble beginning: we will soon start the foundations of the main Museum, which will house exhibitions from the Vedas to the India of tomorrow. If God, in spite of my shortcomings, gives me the strength, the enthusiasm and the dynamism, it will be a wonderful and noble project that will be talked about for centuries. But for that, we need funds, a lot of funds. I hope those of you who will read these words, will be touched and will pass along the message to their friends. This is a Museum of the greatness, tragedy and enduring power of the Hindus. THIS IS A MUSEUM OF HINDU POWER.

FACT is a registered Trust and has US, UK and Indian tax exemption, as well as FCRA. Donations in Indian rupees can be made at the following account:

Foundation Against Continuing Terrorism (FACT)
Account No: 04071450000237. IFCS code: HDFC0000407
Bank Address: HDFC Bank Ltd., T S No.6, 100 Feet Road
Ellaipillaichavadi, Pondicherry-605 005.
Namaste

François Gautier/Trustee FACT (fgautier@rediffmail.com)

Chapter 28

Reciprocity and Hindus

This starts as a beautiful story. Once upon a time, there was a tiny village in South Arcot's district of Tamil Nadu, called Kuilapalayam. Now Kuilapalayam is like hundreds of villages around Pondichery: it is peopled with Hindu *Vanniars*, a caste slightly higher than the untouchables, poor, living off agriculture, usually a few meagre fields of cashew nuts. But then Kuilapalayam just happened to be in the midst of Auroville, the international township, founded by the Mother of Pondichery, based upon the ideals of the great yogi and revolutionary, Sri Aurobindo. Thus Kuilaplayam prospered: its inhabitants learned trades needed for the city: carpenters, masons, craftsmen, some of its children attended Auroville's schools and were educated along with western kids and in time graduated and went into white collar jobs. From a few cycles 40 years ago, Kuilapalayam has today motorcycles, tractors, cars, vans, cable TV, cell phones, etc. The main road of Kuilapalayam which used to be only shady huts, became lined-up with fancy shops which sold everything, from vegetables to handicrafts.

And then the unavoidable happened: a Kashmiri Muslim from Chennai heard about Auroville and the prosperity of Kuilapalaym and understanding that he could make a packet with so many westerners passing though Auroville, he opened the usual shawls and carpets' shop in the village. Now Kuilapalayam never counted a Muslim amongst its population in its 1200 years of recorded history; but in the true Hindu tradition, this one was welcomed and nobody raised an objection, although he was competition for some of the other shops. Our Kashmiri Muslim, seeing his success, called his cousin in

Kolkata, who came and opened another shop; and that one phoned his friend in Mumbai, who also landed-up and opened a third shop. Still nobody found anything to say. Kashmiris are sociable fellows and they quickly made friends with Westerners, most of them blissfully unaware of the political situation in India, so business was booming, till they were seven or eight Kashmiri shops in Kuilapalayam. And again nobody complained, even when the fellows started doing their *naamaz* openly. "Isn't God everywhere and isn't He Krishna, as well as Allah," said one ofthe villagers?

Then Karunan, one of the young boys of Kuilapalayam, who had gone to study in Delhi, told his parents when he came back, about the fact that not only no Hindu were allowed to buy land or start a shop in the Valley of Kashmir, where the shopkeepers came from (this was in 2018, before the abrogation of Article 370), but that four hundred thousand Hindus, were chased out of the Valley by terror, many of them having been murdered and that they were living as refugees in Jammu and Delhi. His parents started talking to their friends and there was the first hint of resentment against the newcomers.

Fifteen days later, a few Hindus going-up to Amarnath were ambushed. Karunan's father went to see a group of Kuilaplayam Kashmiris having tea and told them that Hindus never complained about their government giving billion of rupees in subsidies to Indian Muslims so that they can visit their most Holy place, the Mecca. "But when Hindus, he continued, need shelters, toilets and basic facilities at height of 15,000 feet to worship at Amarnath, one of the holiest places of Hinduism, why do you Kashmiri Muslims even attack us"? The Kashmiris looked a bit uneasy, then replied "that anyway the Amarnath ice lingam had been discovered by a Muslim shepherd and that Muslims had always welcomed their Hindu brothers to Armanath." But this did not convince the Kuilapalayam man who had heard from his son that many grenade attacks had happened over the years against the Amarnath pilgrims. And anger started mounting in Kuilapalayam.

So it is all a question of *reciprocity*. Most Hindus are peace-loving people. The average Hindu that you meet in a million Indian villages, such as Kuilapalayam, is easy-going and accepts you and your diversity, whether you are Christian, Muslim, Parsi or Jain, Arab, French or Chinese. He goes about his business and usually does not interfere in yours.

In fact Hindus take it a little further: they hate trouble and go out of their way to avoid it. Have you noticed how every time there is a possibility of a strike or trouble, Hindus stay home? Or how – forget about rioting – Hindus never speak-up, complain or protest in a united manner. There was a UN Human Rights conference on terrorism in New York a few years ago and the organizers were desperately trying to get Hindu surviving victims of terrorism to testify; but none were willing to come forward for fear of reprisals.

Not only that, but everywhere in the world, Hindus are hounded, humiliated, routed, be it in Fiji where an elected democratic government was twice deposed in an armed coup a few years ago, or in Pakistan and Bangladesh, where Muslims indulge in pogroms against Hindus every time they want to vent their hunger against India (read Taslima Nasreen's book "Lalja"). In Assam, Tripura, or Nagaland, West Bengal, Hindus are being outnumbered by Bangladeshi illegal immigrants and terrorized by pro-Christian separatist groups, such as the Bodos or the Mizos, while local governments often turn a blind eye. Their temples are being taken over in many states like in Kerala or Karnataka, and the donations appropriated by the state governments.

Thus Hindus, who accept everybody, welcome all religions, allow Indians from other parts to trade next to them, as it happened in Kuilapalayam, do not receive in return any gratitude and the same respect. On the contrary, they get mocked at, bombs are planted in their markets, their trains; their temples get attacked, they are chased out of their homelands; television an newspapers make fun of them, their own politicians ostracize them....

Instead of trying to put water overt the fire, instead of appealing for calm and communal harmony, instead of giving us all this eyewash about a 500 year old Dargah mostly patronized by Hindus (but do Muslims visit Hindu temples in return), political leaders, journalists, as well as spiritual leaders, should do well to look at the root cause of Hindu fury, and try to address their demands and frustrations.

Journalists should also do a little bit of introspection and try to think for themselves. It is unfair, as it has been done in Ayodhya and after the Gujarat riots, to put so much blame on Hindus as if they are the worst criminals in the world and the destroyers of Nehruvian secularism. Millions of temples were destroyed in India by Muslim invaders, some of them the most sacred to Hindus, like the Kashi Vishvanath, Krishna's birth temple in Mathura, the rebuilt Somnath temple and the Treta-ka-Thakur temple in Ayodhya, and Hindus hardly ever protested. When they dare to destroy one disused mosque, without any human casualties, what a hullabaloo has been created year after year by journalists, Muslims and secularists. When Islamic militants plant bomb, they kill scores of Hindus every time. Do Hindus plant bombs upon Muslims? Does one journalist dare to say that? How long can Hindus accept everybody get beaten up and receive nothing in return?

CHAPTER 29

The Father of Hindu Power

The Congress always claimed kinship and ownership to the 'Father of the Nation'. Is indeed the Mahatma, whose tremendous personality nobody can deny, the true architect of Indian Independence, as most history books, both Indian and western, are claiming?

Many biographers of Sri Aurobindo have swept under the carpet his role as a leader of the Congress. Yet there are so many accounts of Sri Aurobindo's revolutionary years. Not many people know that originally the Congress was created in December 1885 by an Englishman, A.O. Hume, with the avowed aim to: "Allow all those who work for the national (read British) good to meet each other personally."

Sri Aurobindo was very clear in what was demanded then and today of a leader of India: "What India needs at the moment is the aggressive virtues, the spirit of soaring idealism, bold creation, fearless resistance, courageous attack." How many Indian politicians today fit into that mould, except Narendra Modi?

Sri Aurobindo re-enacted five thousand years later Krishna's message to Arjuna, by allowing his brother Barin to manufacture bombs in his own house and secretly endorsed early assassinations of select Englishmen. This is very rarely mentioned in any of his biographies.

"Sri Aurobindo never ceased to believe that Indians had the right to use violence to topple a government maintained by violence. But how does that tally with the idea we have about spirituality, which we basically associate with non-violence? Hence this enormously important aspect of Sri Aurobindo's life, of protecting the Dharma, of standing for what is good and true and noble, by force, if necessary, is today ignored and not applied to the enemies of modern India. He is truly thus the father of Hindu Power.

We should also dwell on the famous Uttarpara speech, where Sri Aurobindo, after one year in the Alipore jail, clearly defines what he calls the Sanatana Dharma: "Something has been shown to you in this year of seclusion, something about which you had your doubts and it is the truth of the Hindu religion. It is this religion that I am raising up before the world, it is this that I have perfected and developed through the rishis, saints and avatars, and now it is going forth to do my work among the nations. I am raising this nation to send forth my word.... When therefore it is said that India shall rise, it is the Santana Dharma that shall rise. When it is said that India shall be great, it is the Santana Dharma that shall be great."

If we in France had a great man, such as Sri Aurobindo, who was not only as a revolutionary, a yogi, but also a tremendous philosopher and a peerless poet, we would cherish him endlessly. His poetry would be taught to children, his philosophical works would be part of the universities curriculum, books would be written about him, museums built....

But today amongst Indian politicians, everybody quotes conveniently from Gandhi, although nobody applies his ideals of chakra, non-violence, khadi and chakra. Yet, nobody ever mentions Sri Aurobindo, whose sayings of a 100 years ago are still 100% relevant today. Not only is he absent from schools and universities, but in some manuals written by the Congress, he is branded as a 'terrorist'. Shame on India!

Somnath Chaterjee, now defunct, who in his time was made an icon by the Media, in spite of having disobeyed his party and sitting on the cash for votes scam, has built an Indian History museum in the Parliament annexe at a great cost of the tax payer's money. In this museum, which is visited by all school children of Delhi and surrounding states, the history of India more or less starts with Ashoka (because he was supposedly Buddhist), jumps to Akbar (who is glorified beyond measure) and finishes up with Subash Chandra

Bose, Gandhi and Nehru. Not a single mention of Sri Aurobindo oreven Tilak, the true fathers of the nation..

Is it not time that Indian history be rewritten and that we rectify the major injustice done to Sri Aurobindo, the true father of Indian Independence, he who prophetically said about Pakistan in 1947: "India is free, but she has not achieved unity, only a fissured and broken freedom.... The whole communal division into Hindu and Muslim seems to have hardened into the figure of a permanent political division of the country. It is to be hoped that the Congress and the Nation will not accept the settled fact as for ever settled, or as anything more than a temporary expedient. For if it lasts, India may be seriously weakened, even crippled; civil strife may remain always possible, possible even a new invasion and foreign conquest. The partition of the country must go.... For without it the destiny of India might be seriously impaired and frustrated. That must not be."

And the question must be asked: Sri Aurobindo was a Congressman, although he was shunned by his fellow politicians as a radical or an extremist. Cannot the Congress of today at last recognize that Sri Aurobindo was a precursor?

CHAPTER 30

Hindu Power and Hindu Women

Men cannot have power without Shakti. It is thus essential to have a look at the role of Hindu women in India and the importance of their being part of Hindu Power. Most western televisions and newspapers always strive to demonstrate that life for a Hindu in India is the most miserable, the most dangerous, the most deprived, the most unhappy, the most ostracized that one can dream off on this planet.

There was this article claiming that every year, millions of female feticides are killed in India: there was all these statistics on the millions of HIV-infected women, there were numerous articles on child marriage, girls' labor, girl child exploitation and girl sex abuse, rapes, etc.

It's strange, I am lived for nearly fifty years in India and I have traveled the length and breadth of this country, like very few western correspondents have. I am even in close touch with villages of Tamil Nadu, populated only with OBC's and Untouchables. And my experience has been totally – but TOTALLY – different. Yes, there are abuses on women in India, there may be some villages in UP or in some remote tribal belts, where female feticide is practiced; yes, women in India work so hard, toiling in the fields, looking after their children, cooking, cleaning, getting up before dawn and sleeping late; yes, men in India tend to drink a lot and sometimes abuse their wives. But I have never seen any other country where women play such an important role, where she is so worshipped, revered, prized upon – I am talking about Hindu women, of course, not Muslims ones.

Western correspondents are always keen to do stories on female infanticides in Bihar, child marriages, or *sati* cases in Rajasthan. But who knows that no nation in the world has granted such an important place to women in its spirituality and social ethos? "Without Him I exist not, without Her I am unmanifest," says Sri Aurobindo. Thus in India – and it is true that it is often a paradox, as women, because of later Muslim influences, have often been relegated to the background – the feminine concept is a symbol of dynamic realization. She is the eternal Mother, who is all Wisdom, all Compassion, all Force, Beauty and Perfection. It is in this way that since the dawn of times, Hindus have venerated the feminine element under its different manifestations: *Makalaxmi, Mahakali, Mahasaraswati, Maheshwari* – and even India is feminine: 'Mother India'. "She is the consciousness transcending all things, she is the emptiness beyond all emptiness, the smile beyond all smiles, the divine beauty beyond all earthly beauties." India has had many great female figures, whether warriors such as the Rani of Jhansi, or saints like today's Amrita Anandamayi. In the 21th century, behind all appearances – arranged marriages, submission to men, preference of male children in some rural areas (but girls are loved in India like nowhere in the world) – the role of Hindu women in India is essential and it can be safely said that very often, from the poorest to the richest classes, they control – even if behind the scenes – a lot of the family affairs: the education of their children (men in India are often "mama's boys"), monetary concerns, and men often refer to them for important decisions.

How come then this flurry of statistics on every Women's Day, which tend to prove the contrary? Well, if you look closely, you will discover the source of all these statistics. The writer of the piece, claiming millions of female feticides every year, was a Christian working for an NGO, funded by Christian funds (as were many other pieces in leading dailies); there was also a sprinkling of Muslim intellectuals led by Shabana Azmi and her husband, adding their bit about the poor status of women in India and how they are raped, abused and exploited; The communists, under the banner of Brinda Karat, were not far away in loudly denouncing human rights abuses on women in India; the Congress, joined in the chorus, thereby demeaning themselves as Indians and putting down their own country.

Westerners love to preach India on Human Rights. But countries such as France or the United States, never had a woman as their top leader, whereas India had Indira Gandhi ruling with an iron hand for nearly twenty years; and now Sonia Gandhi, a Christian, a Westerner, and just an ordinary MP, is reigning on India like an Empress! The reverse would be absolutely impossible in the West, where there are proportionately less MP's than India, which is considering earmarking 33% of seats in Parliament for women, a revolution in human history! This *shakti* concept is so rooted in the subcontinent, that you have had women Prime Ministers, such as the now deceased Benazir Bhutto or Kaleda Zia, and now Sheikh Hasina, in Islamic countries (Pakistan and Bangladesh) which are predominantly male-controlled in a much stricter way than India. Do you know which countries have the most female airline pilots? United-States? England? France? No, India! Recently an all-female crew pilots and air hostesses flew, a Delhi-San Francisco flight, once of the longest route in the world. Air India again operated 52 flights with all-women crews on Women's Day 2019.

Now who is the target of all these attacks? The Hindus, of course, the common enemy to Christians, Muslims and Marxists! For Christians, Hindus are still all 'pagans' to be converted. Please see the letters written to Sonia Gandhi when her party was in power, by some of the Christian religious leaders of this country after the anti Conversion law was voted by the Himachal Pradesh Government. For Marxists, who believed that religion is the 'Opium of the people', Hinduism is the greatest threat to their planned hegemony on India (and on South Asia, as they are propping-up the Maoists in Nepal, who are now in the Government while retaining their armed stronghold in the country side. One day they will form a Maoist belt from Nepal to Andhra Pradesh, via Bihar). Of course, this Marxist hatred of religion does not apply to Christianity and Islam, who would immediately reply in kind and who are their allies in their war against Hinduism. Right down from Aurangzeb's times, Hindus have been looked upon by Muslims as inferior human beings, although it is better to be born a Hindu woman, where one can go with open face, work, have some amount of freedom, than be born as a Muslim woman.

When Will Hindus start being proud of themselves, their women and their own culture and stop berating themselves and looking down on their own society? This inferiority complex is a legacy of the British, who strove to show themselves as superior and Indian culture as inferior. India is a vast, complex, often contradictory country, peopled with different races, religions, ethnies.... It is normal that there are problems. But women have played and are still playing such an important role in this country, the Shakti concept is such a unique, vibrant, respectful and holy concept, that all Indians, including Indian Christians and Indian Muslims, whose women have somehow benefited from that concept, which seeped into their religion unobtrusively, should be proud of it. Long Live the Indian Woman and her astonishing Grace. Hindu Power needs Hindu women and their Shakti. And today we see that Nirmala Sitaraman, or Smriti Irani, or Maneka Gandhi are very much at the centre of Hindu Power.

CHAPTER 31

Hindu Power Needs a Uniting of All Hindu Gurus

A true Hindu power without the support of Hindu Gurus will not be possible as the great Hindu gurus of today, whether Amrita Anandamayi, Sri Sri Ravi Shankar Jaggi Vasudev, the Shankaracharya, Shri Ramdev, Sai Baba, (although he is no more) etc, hold sway over tens of millions of Hindus. Yet what we have witnessed in the last 50 years is that Hindu gurus tend to distance themselves from Hinduism, so as to appear more 'secular' and attract western (and sometimes Muslim disciples).

The enemies of Hindus are united, even if it is in disunity, even if it is a temporary arrangement based on a common hatred. Christian conversions, the onslaught of Muslim fundamentalism, the abhorrence of communists for Hinduism, the infinite dangers of Globalisation and Americanisation, the disregard of India's intellectual elite of India for their own culture and spirituality, are slowly but surely making a dent in India's psyche....

Yet the Hindu Gurus of India are not only not united against the common enemy, or for the common good, but they often compete against each other for disciples or territory and even criticize each other.

Disunity has always been the curse of Hinduism and India and whichever enemy conquered this country, did it not because of superior strength, but because they were helped by Hindu betrayers. Remember the last great Hindu empire, that of Vijaynagar.

The Christians have a Pope, the Muslims the word of the Koran, communists have Der Kapital of Karl Marx, but Hindus are **fragmented** in a thousand sects, which often bicker with each other.

It is thus of vital importance **that Hindu gurus and swamis regroup under one umbrella**. Each group and guru will retain its leadership and autonomy but will meet three times a year.

There are too many gurus and swamis all over India and the world and it would not be possible to assemble them all in one group. Thus we propose that **the twelve gurus in India** who have the most disciples, represent all the other swamis and gurus. Amongst them of course, we should find Sri Sri Ravi Shankar, Amrita Anandamayi, the Shankacharya of Kancheepuram, Guruma of Ganeshpuri, Shri Ramdev, Satguru Jaggi etc.

The leadership of this group will be rotated every year and so can membership for that matter, as there are quite a few other gurus of India who have a huge following.

It is not only Hinduism which is at stake, but the Knowledge Infinite which came down, through the ages and has survived today only in India in a partial form. **This Knowledge only can save the world.**

FACT-India, which is a non-political, non-partisan, NGO, will provide the umbrella under which all the gurus can meet three times a year and issue a number of 'adesh', which will be binding to 800 million Hindus in India, a billion worldwide. Let Hindus at last understand that not only they have the numbers, but also that they are one of the most successful, law abiding and powerful communities in the world.

Long Live Mother India

CHAPTER 32

Cry O My Beloved India: Look at What Thy Children Have Done to Thee...

At some point, we have to realize that Hindu Power – real Hindu Power – may be a far dream.... When South African Alan Paton wrote 'Cry The Beloved Country' he was lamenting over how the whites can devise, construct and implement race- and colour-based social and economic injustices over the blacks in apartheid-era South Africa. 'Cry O my Beloved India' could be very well applied to today's politics in India, for things have gone to such a pitch of unfair, blatant and outrageous illogical state, that it baffles the mind. Yet neither the politicians, nor most of the press find anything wrong in it.

Sadhvi Pragnya, a Hindu lady monk, languished in jail for months, even though no conclusive proofs were brought forward of her direct involvement in the Malegaon blasts case, and was even assaulted by a Muslim inmate at Byculla Jail and sustained injuries to her face, nose and neck. She may be a MP now, but Narendra Modi said he would never forgive her because of something she said. yet you have the Islamist leader Abdul Nasser Madani, a prime accused in the Coimbatore bomb blasts, which cost the life of 60 people, who stood for election in Kerala with the full backing of the CPI-M. Kerala indeed is becoming a mini Pakistan, where entire districts, like Waynyad were Rahul Gandhi was recently elected an MP, with a rabid Muslim majority.

And what of West Bengal? Mamta Banerjee shamelessly canvasses the Muslim vote by clamping down on Hindus, who have become in minority in many districts, because of the huge illegal

Bangladeshi inflow, which Mamta uses by quickly giving them ration cards, which open the door to voting and even citizenship. The BJP central Govt is quite silent and you need a Tapan Ghosh, a real Hindu Hero to dare stand-up against her and for Hindus. The same if true of Assam where illegal Bangladeshis are persecuting the Hindus, with the state turning a blind eye, in spite of the efforts of the BJP Government to deport some of these illegals.

In Orissa a few years back, the police arrested BJP candidate from Kandhamal constituency, Ashok Sahu, because he accused the Church of using foreign money to induce innocent tribals to convert – which is a very well documented fact, please read Tehelka's cover story.

Yet, terrorist, Kasab, who went on killing people as if he was strolling in a mall, enjoyed a royal life in the entire Arthur jail that had been vacated for him. 11,000 pages of his indictment charges were translated in Urdu, just because the gentleman had asked for it and the court? And the Congress dithered so long before executing him.

In the same way, the Muslim president of India during the 2d Congress term, we shall not name him here, hesitated so long to allow terrorist Memom, who has committed treason against his own country, to be hanged, for fear of alienating the Muslim vote. Yet the Congress keeps telling us that Indian Muslims are patriotic. Then, why did thousands of them in Mumbai attend his funeral?

It is fashionable nowadays to go after Hindu gurus, which the press likes to label as 'godmen' and recently a television channel did a program to show that gurus were interfering in politics. But it is absolutely untrue: not only traditionally Brahmins never meddled in states, contrary to the Christian Church and Islam where the mollah rules, but Hindu gurus today are so disunited that their voice is barely heard.

India is all about equality and rising above castes; yet since 1947, politicians of this country, particularly the Congress, and later V.P. Singh, Mulayam Singh, or Lalu Prasad, have hopelessly divided India along castes and religious lines. But Mayawati tops them all: she tried to give a push to her prime ministerial aspirations, by promising

Scheduled Caste status to 16 more castes if she came to power at the Centre.

In India you are supposed to be elected with ten lakhs of white money. But everybody knows that to become an MP today, you need ten crores, as you have to boast of a hundred cars' caravan when you go campaigning, hire private planes, helicopters, gift free saris, dhotis, televisions, cash even, more and more. So, where do you get the 9 crores and 90 laks black money? From corrupt businessmen, from the mafia, from kickbacks.

The tragedy is that the Indian press does not play its role, because not many mainstream newspapers or television channels complained when Colonel Shrikant Purohit was in jail, falsely accused by the Congress and Chidambaram, while Madani, a criminal who has the lives of 60 innocent people on his hands, was not only scot free, but was standing as an MP with the full backing of a political party, whose leader once said that he will not refuse the post of Prime Minister.

The real problem is that India has been colonized for too long, contrary to China whose people remain proud of their culture and intensely nationalistic. It has resulted, as we keep repeating here, in a deep-rooted inferiority complex in the Indian psyche, whereas every intellectual is always looking towards the West for approval and Indians are so obsessed with having the western type of democracy, without adapting it to the Indian conditions. The system has become so perverted that only radical surgery to remove the diseased parts will start the indispensable cleansing process.

Cry O my beloved India: look at what Thy children have done to Thee... Hindu Power is still far away...

CHAPTER 33

A List of the 50 Biggest Enemies of Hindus (Dead or Alive)

Hindus should at least know who are their enemies; otherwise there never will be real Hindu Power. Jews have shown us that to remember, helps to make sure that atrocities do not happen again. Let us not forget that the biggest genocide ever – is that of the Hindus – which has been calculated at 100 million victims, from the Hindu Kush to the Mumbai attacks of 2006.

This list, which is compiled without any hatred or malice, is not complete. I am counting on you to raise it to a hundred. If you think I missed someone, facebook it to me, with the name and two or three paragraphs on why you think he or she is an enemy of the Hindus.

It would be also interesting to compile separately a list of say, the ten or twenty biggest enemies of Hindus in the US (or UK, or Canada) that could be circulated worldwide and damper the activities of these people....

I have also made a hit parade of the ten countries that I feel are inimical to Hindus.

HERE THE LIST:

1. **Thomas Babington**, 1st Baron Macaulay. Played a major role in introducing English and western concepts to education in India. This was good and one cannot deny that English gives India an edge, say compared to China, in dealing with the West and conducting business. Yet, Macaulay had very little regard for Hindu culture and education: « all the historical information which can be collected from all the books which have been written in the Sanskrit language,

is less valuable than what may be found in the most paltry abridgement used at preparatory schools in England ». Macaulay thus succeeded in fashioning a class of "brown Sahibs", who thought and acted British. Today, much of India's intelligentsia and Media stands proof that Macaulay succeeded: they look down on their own culture and analyse India through the western Prism.

2. Indian National Congress. Few people know that the Indian National Congress was founded on 28 December 1885 by a Britisher, A.O. Hume. Its goals were to « allow all those who work for the national (read British) good to meet each other personally, to discuss and decide of the political operations to start during the year." And certainly, till the end of the 19th century, the Congress, who regarded British rule in India as a "divine dispensation", was happy with criticising moderately the Government, while reaffirming its loyalty to the Crown and its faith in "liberalism" and the British innate sense of justice!!!" Real nationalist leaders like Sri Aurobindo or Tilak, were side-lined by the 'Moderate' Congress'. Today, we find that the British succeeded in implanting an eternal love of the 'White' in the Congress, witness the sycophancy around Sonia Gandhi.

3. Jawarlhal Nehru. Nehru, writes French historian Alain Danielou, "was the perfect replica of a certain type of Englishman. He often used the expression 'continental people', with an amused and sarcastic manner, to designate French or Italians. He despised non-anglicised Indians and had a very superficial and partial knowledge of India. His ideal was the romantic socialism of 19th century Britain. But this type of socialism was totally unfit to India, where the conditions were totally different from 19th century Europe. The Congress has today made an icon out Nehru, which nobody has yet dared to touch, but as History will show more and more, Nehru did tremendous harm to India by initiating movements and patterns, which not only did vast damage in their times, but continue to survive and weigh down the Indian nation, long after their uselessness has been realized.

4. **Babur**. Do you know what Jawaharlal Nehru wrote about Babur the destroyer of the Ram temple in Ayodhya? "Babur did not like India and preferred to isolate himself in the exquisite gardens he had devised, with their geometrical design, their crossed canals, which evoked to him the rivers of paradise." The truth is that Babur was probably the most ferocious Moghol emperor, indulging in unnecessary massacres and that he razed thousands of temples. His ultimate goal was the destruction and the enslaving of the Hindus. It is sad that today Indian History books do not mention his crimes.

5. **Sonia Gandhi**. It is a fact that Sonia brought discipline, order and cohesion into the Congress party. But the amount of power, that she, a non-Indian, a simple elected MP, like hundreds of others, possessed when the Congress was in power for ten years, should frighten us: a word, nay a glance of her was sufficient to trigger action by her entourage, using any means – witness how P. Chidambaram would have allowed Narendra Modi to be killed by a Israt Jahan, a known terrorist. Thus, the instruments of power had never been so perverted in India. The CBI blatantly and shamelessly quashed all injunctions against Quattrochi and even allowed him to get away with billions of rupees which he had stolen from India. Yet, without batting an eyelid, and with the Indian Media turning a blind eye, it went ruthlessly after Narendra Modi, the then Chief Minister of the most efficiently run state, the most corruption free. Sonia Gandhi continues to be a danger to Hindus, because if by some freak chance Modi loses in 2019, as Vajpayee did before him, Sonia will again become the empress of India.

6. **The Pope.** Christianity, unfortunately, is still clinging in the belief of a single true God, Jesus Christ, in spite of the feeble attempts at "Ecumenism" of the Church. In fact as church attendance is dropping drastically in the West, as less and less youth are willing to become priests and nuns and as the Church is shaken by paedophilia scandals, the Pope's call "for the Evangelisation of Asia in the Third Millennium" is a clear indication that, like the Tobacco companies having less customers in the West, the Church is

looking for new converts in the Third World! It would be all right if the Church was playing by the rules of the free market, where there is a certain amount of fairness: "you see what advantages my religion is bringing you, compare it with your own and then feel free to chose." But, sadly, the missionaries are using unethical means to convert the poorest of the poor Hindus in India: offering free medical treatment, free schooling, interest-free loans, even going as far as organizing "fake miracles" prayer meetings, as it is regularly done by American Preacher Benny Hinn. They do it in India, but they dare not do it in China, where freedom of religion is curtailed and any missionary caught proselytising is kicked out. Would Hindus dare convert Christians in France, for instance ? You are joking : there is not a single Hindu temple in France, as their construction has not been allowed and there is even a minister in charge of hunting down "sects" (meaning what is not Christian-oriented).

7. Rahul Gandhi. No doubt Rahul Gandhi is a decent, well meaning man, though totally ignorant of India's culture and spirituality as his father was. But his ignorance makes him a dangerous man. Remember the Wikileaks cables, where Rahul Gandhi tells the American ambassador that Hindu terrorism was more dangerous than Islamic terrorism: *"The bigger threat may be the growth of radicalized Hindu groups, which create religious tensions and political confrontations with the Muslim community."* It seems also that Rahul and his mother wanted to make an example of Colonel Purohit and Sadhvi Pragya to please their Muslim electorate and that direct orders were issued from 10 Janpath to get a confession out of him and Sadhvi Pragya at any cost, even torture. Good that he has resigned as President Congress.

8. The Communist Party of India. Very few people know that the communists refused to collaborate against the Nazis during the 2d World War, because Russia was then allied with Germany. Their attitude during the war with China in 1962 was also very ambivalent and today newspapers like the Hindu or Frontline are just mouthpieces of the Chinese points of view. Most Marxists in India are anti-Hindu as a principle (Marx was against religion) and their intellectuals are adept at Hindu bashing. Ata time when Marxism is dead all over the world, including in Cuba and China, India is the last refuge of communism. Though communists have a certain sincerity (they generally are not corrupt and live a simple life, contrary to many Indian politicians), it is not a gift to India, as they contribute very little to India's growth, with their constant strikes and demands. Naxalism which is a great danger for this country is also an offshoot of communism.

9. Pryanka Gandhi. Nobody wants to bother Priyanka Gandhi as long as she leads her life, raises her children and is an Indian like another India. But in case her mother Sonia leaves India or something happens to her, Priyanka – and not Rahul – will be the natural choice of the Congress to take up the reins. Would Priyanka think and act differently from her mother, brother, father and grandfather ? Unlikely. She will think like a Christian and a westerner, not like an Indian and adopt Nehru's misplaced socialist and popular idea's, which have bogged down India in corruption and red tape. Plus her husband Robert Vadra, a man who multiplied his wealth by 600 in five years, is an albatross around her neck. Will she take over the post of President Congress?

10. Barkha Dutt. Most probably Barkha (who has today left NDTV) started like a young and idealistic journalist. But the fact that she was married twice to a Kashmiri Muslim, must have influenced her mind. The power that came with NDTV, as it grew into the most sophisticated TV news channel, and her proximity to the Congress party, also went to her head. From a young journo, Barkha turned into a Hindu basher – you just have to listen to the Radia tapes to understand that. Also, woe to those who disagree with her in her interviews and programs, as she rudely interrupts them when she feels like it. There are also accusations of corruption against her and her ex boss Prannoy Roy.

11. Kancha Ilaiah. Known for his immensely controversial book, 'Why I am not a Hindu', Kancha Ilaiah, is a converted

Christian, who hates Hindus, particularly Brahmins, whom he accuses of all the possible evils. This hatred makes him irrational. For instance, he recently said that vegetarianism is anti-nationalism: "For me, my nation starts with eating beef. Unfortunately, we gave up eating beef and our brains are not growing now. There is no enough protein," ... How stupid can you be, when many westerners are now turning to vegetarianism?

12. Aamir Khan. Once upon a time, Aamir Khan, benefited from the goodwill of all, Muslims as well as Hindus. His TV program on social issues, Satyamev Jayata, even raised his status to a crusader for human rights. Then slowly the mask dropped, and one could see that he was no different from the average Muslim, when it came to Hindus, the BJP and Narendra Modi. His reflection on 'Intolerance ' and that his (Hindu) wife wanted to leave India, alienated him from many of his supporters. His anti-Hindu gurus film, like PK, created too a lot of enmity. Not a friend of Hindus. Pity that he is courted by the PM, against whom he had signed a petition when Modi was CM Gujarat.

13. Shah Rukh Khan. As Aamir Khan, Shah Rukh is also married to a Hindu, but raises his kids as Muslims, and whenever it suits him, plays the minority card (Pakistan invited him many times to settle there). What one should understand is that it is like elections in India: Aamir's and Shah Rukh's Muslim fan base in India is so huge, that they don't really care about Hindus. In fact, playing a little anti-Hindu card, pleases their Muslim fans and does no harm to their image, as Hindus anyway never retaliate, even by boycotting their films.

14. Amartya Sen. This one is a deadly enemy of Hindus, much more than many, because he got the Nobel Prize, teaches in Oxford and is highly respected in the West. But make no mistake about it: Amartya Sen is a true Marxist and he rode his fame on the back of his false theories about poverty in India and in the West. It is a pity that the Congress Government gave him the Nalanda University project for which he did nothing. He should become persona non grata in India.

15. Rajdeep Sardesai. Rajdeep is a nasty guy and not an honest journalist – witness the incident when he sat on a sting interview that showed the Congress paying bribes to BJP MLA's to defect. He was also seen in his true light in New York, where he portrayed himself as a victim of a hard-line Hindu, whereas the video replays showed that in fact he was the aggressor. No doubt, Rajdeep is a personal enemy of Narendra Modi and has never hid his dislike of the BJP. There have been many rumours that his father, converted to Christianity late in life and that may have influenced Rajdeep, for he has definitely a Christian-Marxist view of India and Hindus.

16. Angana Chatterjee. Angana Chatterjee, is one of the most venomous anti-Hindu in the USA. The irony is that she is a Hindu herself and started in an association named after India's avatar, himself a great defender of Hindus, Sri Aurobindo. You need to know that she is married to Richard Shapiro who is Director and Associate Professor of the Grad. Anthropology Program at CIIS, also a very anti-Hindu body. In fact, Shapiro was barred from entering India in 2010. Angana and Richard are of course great defenders of the Kashmiri Muslims and attend every International Kashmir Freedom Conference (IKFC), which only gives the Muslim point of view and ignores the 450.000 Kashmiri Hindus who have become refugees in their own country.

17. Teesta Setalvad. First it should be known that Teesta is a Hindu herself, who like Barkha Dutt, is married to a Muslim, Javed Anand. Javed, is General Secretary of Muslims for Secular Democracy, a virulent anti-Hindu organization. Using her organization Teesta Setalvad's name has come to symbolize everything that is wrong with NGO activism in India. She has used any means to go after Hindus, particularly their leaders and specially Narenda Modi. Unfortunately, Teesta has been repeatedly exposed for having indulged in unethical acts and has cases pending against her in courts for perjury. The truth is that Teesta Setalvad is a law unto herself and has total disregard for the rule of law or for victims.

Her anti-Hindu agenda is her source of income from foreign agencies. She has taken the courts for a ride with her perjury and her acts of influencing witnesses. She has misused the lack of education and poverty of victims to file false affidavits to further her own agenda.

18. Aurangzeb. Aurangzeb was a monster not only to Hindus, but also to his own family: he beheaded his brother Dara Shikoh, who was the rightful heir to the throne, poisoned his own father, imprisoned his son.... Yet, Romila Thapar, Harbans Mukhia and Bipan Chandra, once upon a time professors at the JNU in New Delhi, the Mecca of secularism and negationism in India, denied the Aurangzeb genocide on Hindus by replacing it instead with a conflict of classes. What are the facts? Aurangzeb (1658-1707) did not just build an isolated mosque on a destroyed temple, he ordered ALL temples destroyed, among them the Kashi Vishvanath, Krishna's birth temple in Mathura, the rebuilt Somnath temple on the coast of Gujurat, the Vishnu temple replaced with the Alamgir mosque now overlooking Benares and the Treta-ka-Thakur temple in Ayodhya.... Thank God Shivaji Maharaj, a true Hindu hero brought him to his knees. Yet Shivaji is treated as a nobody in Indian History books and Aurangzeb like a stern but just emperor....

19. John Dayal The most virulent and articulate Christian anti-Hindu, John and many other Indian Christian leaders and bishops, is not only practicing a Christianity which had its place 50 years ago in Europe (but is no more today, as Western Christianity is evolving), but are also re-embracing the old colonial missionary concept that Christ is the only 'true' God and that all 'heathens' Hindus have to be converted. John Dayal is all the time lobbying in the West, particularly with the US Congress, testifying that 'Christians are persecuted in India', whereas actually Christians have been the worst persecutors in the world, wiping out ruthlessly entire cultures, like those of the Aztecs in South America.

20. Irfan Habib, At last, Irfan Habib have been side-lined by the Modi Government! He and Romila Thapar ruled supreme for nearly 40 years in devising Indian school curriculum. Together they have falsified Indian History with total impunity and went after the Hindus full steam. Irfan Habib continued the legacy of his father, Mohamed Habiib, to rewrite the Chapter of Muslim invasions in India. Habib father and son's books are based on four theories: (1) that the records (written by the Muslims themselves) of slaughters of Hindus, the enslaving of their women and children and razing of temples were "mere exaggerations by court poets and zealous chroniclers to please their rulers." (2) That they were indeed atrocities, but mainly committed by Turks, the savage riders from the Steppe. (3) That the destruction of the temples took place because Hindus stored their gold and jewels inside them and therefore Muslim armies plundered these. (4) That the conversion of millions of Hindus to Islam was not forced, "but what happened was there was a shift of opinion in the population, who on its own free will chose the Shariat against the Hindu law (Smriti), as they were all oppressed by the bad Brahmins"…!!!

21. **Ramachandra Guha**, Outlook magazine's favourite columnist, is a renowned Hindu/Hindu gurus/Hindu culture hater, who like Rahul Gandhi, recently said that "Hindu fundamentalism is more threatening than Islamic terrorism." He has written a number of books targeting Hindus and their spiritual leaders. Unfortunately, as many of these leftist intellectuals, he is fairly popular in the West and often quoted by western correspondents based in India.

22. **Romilla Thapar.** The most renowned Indian historian, who has links with all Indologists in the world, universities and India centers. As Rajiv Malhotra writes: "Hindu spiritual experiences are devalued by Romila Thapar, as pathological. She resorts to a quasi-scholarly speculation of racial hatred as existing in entire Indian traditions, demonizing the 'other', a technique to justify holding such people in contempt and even attacking them." This is exactly the same thesis that is being spread today by Maoist insurgents working among remote tribes in central India, namely, that demons

mentioned in Hinduism are actually references to tribal people ». Today even, most of the intellectuals, journalists and many of India's elite have been influenced by that school of thinking and regularly ape its theories. Romila Thapar is a traitor to her own culture and society, for she is a Hindu.

23. N Ram and the Hindu newspaper. Long time editor of the newspaper the Hindu, who should be renamed the "Anti-Hindu." N. Ram is a fervent disciple of Marxism and communist China. The magazine of the Hindu, Frontline, although well written, as the Hindu, perpetuates a dead ideology. Unfortunately, the Hindu is still read by many in India, including westerners in the South of India.

24. Sagarika Ghose and CNN IBN, Rajdeep Sardesai's wife shares his beliefs and hatred for the Hindus. It's a tragedy that CNN IBN is so partial towards Hindus and sympathetic to anybody who is anti-Hindu. Why did CNN, a renowned western television, choose to partner someone who is against the majority community of their country?

25. Mamta Banerjee. It is said that Mamta Banerjee is a Kali worshipper and does regular pujas when she is alone in her house. Unfortunately Mamta has realized that she can get elected as West Bengal Chief Minister on the sole strength of the Muslim vote. She thus panders to them, turning a blind eye to the atrocities committed on the Hindus by the Bangladeshis refugees, who are given ration cards so that they can vote for Mamta. Sad also that she chose to say 'Allah O Akbar' when she just got re-elected. To what depths will Indian politicians sink to get votes? Hindus are becoming minorities in certain districts of WB, Assam or UP. That is a tragedy and something should be done.

26. Akbaruddin Owasi. Proof that India is a democracy lies in the fact that people like Owasi and his brother can not only rant against the Hindus and preach near secession, but also get elected and re-elected. There has to be some limits to preaching hatred and separatism.

27. Geelani and other Kashmiri separatists. How could the Congress Government allow these separatists to openly visit the Pakistani embassy in Delhi or travel to Pakistan to take instructions from their masters? No country tolerates that kind of open separatism, be it France with Corsica, or even England with the faraway Falkland Islands, which geographically belong to Argentina. How to forget too that the Muslims chased out of the Valley of Kashmir 350,000 Hindus who had lived there for generations and had not done any harm? Good that the Government has finally jailed some of them.

28. Zakir Naik. Zakir Naik tried to hurt religious sentiments of Hindus by denigrating Shri Ganesh; that too, during the Ganesh Festival. He has given a challenge to Hindus, through the medium of 'Facebook' and 'You-tube', to prove that Shri Ganapati is a Deity. He also made an anti-Hindu statement that 'If your God is unable to recognise his own son, how will he know that I am in danger'. By making such comments Naik has hurt religious sentiments of billions of Hindus. It has also created rage among members of Shiv Sena, BJP and various pro-Hindu organisations, Ganeshotsava Mandals and devout Hindus. Naik also went after Sri Sri Ravi Shankar in the famous debate. Great too that he has been exiled.

29. Christophe Jaffrelot. This most famous French Indologist, paid by the French Government, who wrote many a nasty books on 'Hindu fundamentalism' and is most responsible for the bad image of the BJP in France. Funnily, he regularly comes to India to release the English translations of his books and is feted by the Press corps and gets all kind of laudatory reviews. So much for secularism in India_ Jaffrelot, Sanjay Subramanyam (who teaches in the prestigious College de France), and others in France – keep harping on India's problems – castes, poverty, so called-Hindu fundamentalism, etc. I know for a fact that in France, it has an influence on the top bureaucrats and the politicians, as every time something important happens in India – elections, catastrophes, riots, etc, their slanted opinions are sought by newspapers radios and televisions.

30. NGO's. NGO's in India are most of the time anti-Hindus. 70% of them work on "woman empowerment", or "uplifting" the villagers in tribal areas, which is good, but should be done in a neutral manner with friendliness to the Indian Govt. It is nowadays fashionable in India to always highlight the downtrodden condition of Indian women and their underprivileged place in Indian society. But no country in the world has granted such an important place to women in its spirituality and social ethos. And even today, behind all appearances – arranged marriages, submission to men, preference of male children in some rural areas (but girls are loved in India like nowhere in the world) – it can be safely said that very often, from the poorest to the richest classes, women control – even if behind the scenes – a lot of the family affairs: the education of their children (men in India are often "mama's boys"), monetary concerns, and husbands often refer to them for important decisions. Countries such as France or the United States, who are often preaching India on "women's rights" never had a woman as their top leader, whereas India had Indira Gandhi ruling with an iron hand for nearly twenty years; and proportionately they have less MP's than India, which is considering earmarking 33% of seats in Parliament for women, a revolution in human history! But this obsession of NGO's with women and village empowerment (usually they take one village and make it like a showcase, for the benefit of visiting donors from abroad) has completely eclipsed the burning issue that would require NGO's attention with the tremendous amount of funds they attract from abroad : afforestation, as there are hardly any forest worth the name left today in India. Big crackdown on NGO's at moment, but as usual, the lower and middle bureaucracy target also the honest and pro-Indian NGO's.

31. Karunanidhi. Karunanidhi, who died recently, and before him his mentor, Anna, exploited to the hilt he Dravidian theory and he and Anna have made life for Tamil Brahmins so miserable that many left Tamil Nadu for Delhi or even the US. His son Stalin will most like become CM of Tamil Nadu at the next state elections. Though he is a more decent man, he will probably adapt the same anti-Hindu policies.

32. Wendy Doniger. This American Hindu hater, supposedly, a historian, says that "Rama thinks that sex is putting him in political danger (keeping his allegedly unchaste wife will make the people revolt), but in fact he has it backward: Politics is driving Rama to make a sexual and religious mistake; public concerns make him banish the wife he loves. Rama banishes Sita as Dasharatha has banished Rama. Significantly, the moment when Rama kicks Sita out for the second time comes directly after a long passage in which Rama makes love to Sita passionately, drinking wine with her, for many days on end; the banishment comes as a direct reaction against the sensual indulgence. Her latest book, "The Hindus: An Alternative History' was written intentionally to mock Hinduism.

33. Akbar. Akbar is one of the goody-goodies in Indian History books, like Ashoka because he was a Buddhist, that Marxist historians like to glorify. No doubt, Akbar was one of the better Mughal emperors, but did you know that when he captured Chittor on February 25, 1568, he ordered that the thirty thousand civil population be butchered, including women and children who has taken shelter in the fort? Destruction of temples also took place on mass scale in Akbar's reign and it is even said that he ordered that a mountain be made of the tufts of the Brahmins' hairs.

34. Michael Witzel, Professor of Sanskrit at Harvard, Witzel must be one of the worst enemies of Hindus in the USA, as shown recently when he tried to prevent the removal of references to India, Hinduism in the curriculum followed by schools in California which parents of Indian origin found to be inadequate, inaccurate or just outright insensitive. Known for aggressively pushing theories forged by Left historians of the Romila Thapar genre that have been long discredited through scientific means, including DNA studies, this 'linguist' is known for promoting himself as a 'historian' in academic circles. His proximity to Left historians in India is no secret. Such is Prof Witzel's contempt for Indians who live and work in the US that he has not minced words running them down as an ethnic group. On one occasion, he declared: "Hindus in the US are lost or abandoned people."

35. Amnesty International. Amnesty International, which has a large number of Pakistanis in its staff, has always been hostile to Hindus. I remember showing an exhibition on Kashmir in London at the prestigious Commonwealth Club. The south Asia Amnesty in charge, refused to come and see it – although the Club was just a stone throw away from Amnesty's London office. What did the Kashmiri Hindus do that Amnesty considers them untouchable? And how come that the Muslims of the Valley who chased them by terror and made them flee their ancestral lands and homes are not condemned by Amnesty? It triggers a lot of questions about Amnesty's impartiality....

36. Prannoy Roy (CEO of NDTV) No doubt, Prannoy Roy created one of the best TV channels in India, in term of content and professional quality, but from the beginning, NDTV's slant was anti-Hindu. Why? Did you know that Prannoy is married to Radhika Roy, who is the sister of Brinda Karat, one of the leading lights of the communist party of India (CPI(M))? The sad thing is that many BJP leaders always run to NDTV, to be crucified by Barkha Dutt, Pranno's second in command today.

37. Chidambaram. There are many questions asked today about the role of P Chidambaram when he was in power during the ten years of the Congress. As Finance Minister, he went after Hindus by clamping down on Hindu institutions that had the 100% yoga tax rebate; as Home minister, his role is even more dubious: he had cleared an affidavit in 2009 which described college student Ishrat Jahan as a Lashkar-e-Taiba terrorist involved in a plot to assassinate then Gujarat chief minister Narendra Modi. About a month later, a second affidavit was filed in court in which all references to Ishrat's alleged terror links were missing. Did Chidambaram, with the knowledge of Sonia Gandhi close his eyes on an assassination plot on the person of Narendra Modi? As the Home Minister of India, it would be a crime. As this book goes to press, Chidambaram is in jail as this book goes to press and has started atoning for his misdeeds.

38. Sitaram Yechury. Yechury is an intelligent man and a brilliant speaker – but he is an enemy of Hindus. He for instance went full steam against Mr Modi's declaration of June 21 as International Yoga, which was supported by the UN General Assembly and which should not cause any problem, as yoga is a universal technique that is practiced all over the world, by millions of Christians. Oh, but the hitch is that Yoga is a Hindu invention – hence Mr Yechury's hostility, who famously said: "under this BJP government's aggressive global campaigns, India appears to be seeking a global positioning not on the basis of its internal strength, economic or otherwise, but on the basis of such 'accomplishments' as having the UN General Assembly declare International Yoga Day on June 21." The fact that a senior communist leader in India fails to see the potential to leverage the acceptance and spread of Yoga across the world as a means to further India's global influence and power is a testament to the monumental intellectual bankruptcy inflicting the communists in India.

39. Mother Teresa. Mother Teresa is still the worst publicity for India. No doubt, she did saintly work. This said, one may wonder: What did Mother Teresa really stand for? Was caring for the dying and orphaned children her only goal? Mother Teresa never attempted to counterbalance this negative image of India, of whom she was the vector, by a more positive one. She could have said for instance that she was worshipped in a country of 800 million Hindus. The truth is that she stood for the most orthodox Christian conservatism. There is no doubt that ultimately Mother Teresa's goal was utterly simple: to convert Hindus to Christianity, the only true religion in her eyes.

40. Karan Thapar. Karan Thapar, who owns ITV, which unfortunately produces shows for BBC, is one of the most famous faces of journalism in India. Karan Thapar's father was General Pran Nath Thapar COAS during 1962 war, and his aunt is Romila Thapar. Does that explain why Karan, though a decent man, is known for his anti-Hindu bias? Once he invited me on a program about the painter M.F. Husain, who as you know has depicted Hindus' most revered Gods fornicating or even sodomizing each other. I had brought on the show photocopies of these paintings, a solid evidence of Husain's hatred of Hinduism, but Karan refused that I showed them on camera. So much for ITV's journalistic impartiality ... Fortunately, his influence is on the wane.

41. Javed Akhtar. Though Javed Akhtar came out recently against those who opposed saying 'Bharat Mata Ki jai', he is also known as a Hindu baiter. I remember him going full steam against Sri Sri Ravi Shankar and Hindu gurus in an Indian Today symposium a few years ago. Akhtar also repeatedly equated the Gujarat 2002 anti-Muslim riots to the Jewish holocaust. As one of his detractors said: "it is impossible to believe that Akhtar isn't aware of the horrors at Auswitz or Sobibor to compare them with rioting in Gujarat?" Does Alhtar also ignore that 56 innocent Hindus, amongst them 32 women and children were burnt to death like animals in the Sabarmati Express at Godhra? And that this was the spark that ignited the riots? Again, we see how anti-Hindus twist facts and truth....

42. Shabana Azmi. Aktar's second wife, Shabana Azmi is a fine actress. Nevertheless she is also a Hindu baiter. When she was invited to the international film festival of Deauville in France, I read the numerous interviews where she kept harping about "Hindu fundamentalists", and repeatedly lambasted the "Right Wing" BJP Government and accused them of turning a "blind eye" to the attacks towards India's minorities, while portraying herself as a courageous social activist fighting for freedom of expression. She also only spoke "en passant" about Muslim fundamentalism. Again the old trick to either equate Muslim and Hindu fundamentalism, or even in the case of Azmi, Rahul Gandhi and others, to say that Hindu fundamentalism is more dangerous than the Islamic one. What a joke....

43. Akar Patel. Akar Patel, a subtle but redoubtable Hindu hater, was sadly for some time the head of Amnesty International India (one can see there the perversion of Amnesty, to name a Muslim as its head in a country inhabited by 80% Hindus). Akar indeed always rants against Narendra Modi and the Hindu majority, saying: "one must be neutral." but "we dissent against our own country, because dissent is patriotic." However he adds: "Anyone opposing us (Amnesty International?), is morally deficient and a repugnant human being." Akar Patel's virulent hatred for the majority community is not masked. He wrote: "Most extremists in India are not Muslims, they are Hindu Maoists."

44. Arundhati Roy. Cousin of Pranoy Roy, she was married to Gerard Da Cunha first and than to film maker Pradip Kirishen. Arundhati is a pure product of Christianity hiding under an intellectual mask plus hard-core Marxism. Apart from her first book the 'God of Small things', Arundhati never wrote again anything of value. She is most happy in the company of maoists, naxalites Tamil Elam and Kashmiri separatists. Roy famously said: "Kashmir has never been an integral part of India and the Indian Govt is at war with Maoists to aid the MNCs." She also says Modi is promoting Brahmanism. After the "intolerance" debate, she returned her National award for screenplay.Nobody cared....

45. Father Cedric Prakash. This Indian Christian priest has been most active in betraying his own country in the US, amongst Congress parliamentary committees. In June 2002, he testified before the US Commission for International Religious Freedom (USCIRF) in Washington, so about the lack of religious freedom in India.... His is a clear case of an Indian citizen asking an alien nation tintervene in India's domestic affairs. Fr. Prakash has been a vocalcritic of Narendra Modi, often in collaboration with John Dayal and nTeesta Setalvad.

46. Martha Nussbaum. A virulent anti-Hindu American, no doubt supported by Anjana Chatterjee and her ilk. Her pronouncement: "perpetrators of violence are not Muslims but Hindus," is proof enough of that. Her interest in India started while working for Amartya Sen, with whom she shared an intimate relationship, a fact she herself bragged about. Before the 2014 Parliament elections, Amartya Sen had said that he wouldn't like Modi to be the PM of India. Martha does not have any qualification or training in archaeology, Sanskrit, geology, or metallurgy, yet writes with authority about the dating of the Vedas.

47. Hillary Clinton. Hillary Clinton has no great love for India and often leans towards Pakistan (her vice chairman of the 2016 election campaign is Huma Mahmood Abedin, of Pakistani origin). Maybe the numerous infidelities of her husband Bill, made her into a hard and cynical woman, luckily she did not become President of the US, as she would have been no friend of India and Hindus. Her attitude towards Islam and Muslim fundamentalism is also ambiguous and she is probably closer to Obama's views, than any other presidential candidate. You can expect continuing support, financial and in armaments to Pakistan if she is elected.

48. Medha Patkar. Another NGO, who very selectively targets only Hindus. Her Narmada dam agitation had one target only: Narendra Modi. Yet the dam has proved to be the biggest factor to Gujarat's prosperity, bringing electricity, water, prosperity to all, Hindus as well as Muslims. Medha was also involved in many movements that blocked Modi's visas in the UK and the US and that tried to stop him from becoming Prime Minister.

49. The Mahatma Gandhi? I put it with a question mark, as I consider him as a great soul indeed. But there are many who point out that he never seemed to have realised the great danger that Nazism represented for humanity. Calling Hitler "my beloved brother," a man who murdered 6 million Jews in cold-blood just to prove the purity of his own race, is more than just innocence, it borders on criminal credulity. And did not Gandhi also advise the

Jews to let themselves be butchered? ... His not condemning Muslims during the Khalifat movement when thousands of Hindus were butchered by Indian Muslims, or his indulgence of Jinnah, going as far as proposing to make him the Prime Minister of India, have not always earned him Hindu goodwill.

Gandhi's love of the Harijans, as he called them, was certainly very touching and sprang from the highest motivations, but once more Gandhi took the European element in the decrying of the caste system, sowing the seeds of future disorders and of a caste war in India, of which we see the effects only today.

50. HINDUS THEMSELVES. Hindus, as we explain in a earlier chapter, are their own biggest enemies. They must be some of the most selfish and individualistic people in the world: rich Hindus never help their poorer brothers and sisters – that's' why the Mother Teresa's and Sonia Gandhis are able to flourish in India. A Hindu abroad never acknowledges another Hindu, but pretends he or she does not exist. You can insult Hindus and their Gods and Goddesses as much as you want and nothing will happen to you. A billion Hindus have not raised a finger about the 350,000 Kashmiri Pandits who became refugees in their own country after they were chased out by terror from the Valley of Kashmir in the 90's. Hindus today don't give a damn whether their children know about the Ramayana, the Mahabharata or the Bhagavad Gita, where every truth that needs to be known about life, after life, karma, dharma and soul is taught. Modern Hindu children do not go to temples, pray or know what is a puja. Hindus do not care to have colleges where Hindu values are imparted, like the Muslims have (Aligarh university for instance) The only one ever, the Benares Hindu University, should not be called 'Hindu', as nothing Hindu is taught there anymore.

Chhatrapati Shivaji Maharaj, who alone with a few hundred men, stood his ground against the most powerful emperor of his times, has practically no place in Indian History books and is often described as a petty chieftain or even a plunderer. So is Maharana

Pratap, the ONLY Rajput who fought against the Moguls and actually defeated Akbar in Hadilgathi.

Hindus who tend to merge and melt wherever they live – and in the process, lose some their identities and togetherness. And finally the most deadly and vicious intellectuals that we have reviewed above, are Hindus most of them. They are the ones that should be targeted, in a non-violent but firm manner.

COUNTRIES

1. **China**. After seven decades of bitter experience at the hands of the Chinese (see chapter below), of double talk, betrayal and contempt, – India still gets hoodwinked by the Chinese. The reason for this is that the Chinese, who are probably among the most intelligent people in the world, have always understood that India is their number one economic, military and nuclear competitor in Asia (remember how China blocks India's accession to the UN's Security Council, which France supports). The BJP Govt is as prone to succumb to the Chinese 'stick and carrot' policy as the Congress. It's a pity that India does not use the one weapon that rattles the Chinese: the Dalai lama and the Tibetan cause....

2. **Pakistan**. Pakistan is the continuing incarnation of those Muslim invaders who raped India from the middle of the 7th century onwards. Has anything changed: "their cry is still the same: "Dar-ul-Islam", the house of Islam. Yesterday they used scimitars, today they have the atomic bomb; but the purpose is identical, only the weapons have evolved: to conquer India, to finish what the Mughal Emperors were not able to achieve." To reason with Pakistan is useless, many conclude, "for once again they are only putting in practice what their religion teaches them every day – that 'the Pagans shall burn forever in the fire of hell. They are the meanest of creatures.' Or 'Slay the infidels, wherever ye find them and take them captive and besiege them and prepare them for all kinds of ambush.' Or again: 'Choose not thy friends among the Infidels till they forsake their homes and the way of idolatry. If they return to

paganism then take them whenever you find them and kill them.' All these quotations are taken from the Koran and are read everyday to the faithful by their mollahs. (Koran 98:51-9:5-4:89)

3. Bangladesh. In 1947, Muslims constituted only 70% of Bangladesh and Hindus, as well as Christians and Buddhists more than 30%, Today, Muslims are nearly 90 percent, making Bangladesh one of the largest Muslim countries in the world and Hindus, have shrunk to 7%. Successive governments have seized 2.5 million acres of land of the Hindus by using a racist law called the Enemy Property Act (renamed *Vested Property Act* by the secularists). Although finally this racist law was repealed, Khaleda Zia's government has blocked its implementation (*Country Report on Human Rights Practices* – 2001, 2003, *US Department of State*).

Through the 5th and 8th Amendments of the constitution the BNP and JP governments, virtually transformed the once secular Bangladesh into an Islamic state. Apart from money laundering and providing terrorists sanctuary, Bangladesh's madrasas have become major recruiting and training centres for militancy. A CIA study says that Bangladeshi villagers are increasingly getting sucked into terrorism out of livelihood. The very porous border between India and Bangladesh is used as an infiltration route of militants to India, including those going to Kashmir and to the Northeast. The Indian Intelligence Bureau estimates that twenty million Bangladeshis live illegally in India, with the greatest concentration in West Bengal and Assam and this is creating havoc to the social, religious and cultural fabric of the North-East. Chief ministers, such as Mamta Banerjee routinely give rations cards to these illegal Bangladeshis so that they can vote. In West Bengal and Assma, Hindus have become minorities in certain districts are regularly beaten up, their temples ransacked, their women raped. Very few Hindus leaders have taken up their cause, save for Tapan Ghosh in WB.

4. Nepal. Sonia Gandhi, whose government was propped-up by communists, did great damage to India's interests, such as helping a Maoist government come to power in Nepal, the only Hindu state in the world. Here is a wonderful country, with simple and friendly people, which is the only Hindu nation in the world, which is so similar in many ways to India, that there is no reason to be antagonistic to a country with which they have so much in common. Yet the erstwhile kings and now the Maoist leaders in power, are often been able to play a divide and rule game by using the Chinese and blaming India for all the ills of Nepal which as become a haven for Pakistani agents. Today the Maoists are more less in power in Nepal and Chinese presence formidable

5. United-States. The United States, seems sometimes to have an unconscious wish for a divided and weakened India. And did not Senator Galbraith say after the exploding of Yugoslavia that "India is next"? Right now, President Trump, is putting immense pressure on India to negotiate with Pakistan and to do major concessions on Kashmir, which will endanger India's integrity, as Kashmir is such a sensitive strategic state. The continuing propping up and arming of Pakistan, when its duplicity is so well document today, is also a mystery. One does not understand too how so many US Congress committees keep saying that there is no religious freedom in India, when there is actually more freedom here than in the USA. Luckily the Spratly Islands dispute has brought the US and India slightly closer. But there is still a long way to go before the USA really appreciates what an island of democracy and freedom India is in an Asia racked by Muslim fundamentalism, Christian unethical conversions and Chinese domination. Trump is certainly more friendly to India than Obama, but his ignorance of India is abysmal.

6. Afghanistan. India is making great efforts to befriend Afghanistan, so as to balance Pakistan's efforts, which props up the Taliban. But as soon as the US fully leaves this region, Afghanistan will go back to its wild Islamic ways and target India again. It's a pity that once Afghanistan was part of a great Hindu empire and at sometimes too Buddhist.

7. Sri Lanka. Extraordinary country that erstwhile Ceylon; God gave it everything: extraordinary climate, lush country, incredible diversity of races and religions, an easy-going and friendly people, who even welcomed its invaders. Yet the hate that the Sinhalese have for Indians is something to be seen to be believed. Again, it is a hate which was fostered by their political leaders: Most Sinhalese presidents have become great adepts at using the hate-India carrot every time they get in trouble. And why should India be blamed for Sri Lanka's ills? Was it India who discriminated for 40 years against the Tamil minority of Sri Lanka? Was it Indians who regularly prodded Sinhalese crowds to indulge in pogroms against the Tamils, thereby building-up a wall of hatred, so that today the Tamils in Sri Lanka cannot trust the Sinhalese anymore and want nothing but total independence? Today, the LTTE has been apparently wiped out, but make no mistake, the Tamil-Sinhalese divide will reappear under some form or the other. Today the Chinese have more or less bought Sri Lanka and India is surrounded by hostile pro-Chinese countries, from Nepal to Burma.

8. England. When Mountbatten left India with the British flag, ending three centuries of colonization, he made sure that India was permanently divided by propping-up Pakistan and establishing a foreign policy of always putting India and Pakistan on the same foot – policy that was taken-up by the US and Europe. Hindus were the British colonizer's biggest enemy, that is why they also propped up Sikhs, Christians and Muslims to divide India. The birth of Khalistan can be traced to the British. Finally, the British looted Hindu India and stole million of priceless artefacts which are still found in British Museums.

9. Canada. Canada is a subtle enemy of Hindus, solely because it has a huge Sikh population. The Canadians allowed them to breed separatism which led to the Air India Kanishka tragedy. Even then the Canadian government continued to show leniency to the Sikhs and today Trudeau does the same by having a Sikh minister and many Sikh MP's who are friendly to the Khalistani cause.

10. Norway has been a backer of the Naxalite movement and the LTTE for a long time. These are mostly NGO's and individuals, who often come to spend sometimes in villages of Andhra Pradesh or Bihar, to 'uplift' villagers, but have the tacit backing of their Government. It's amazing also how Norway gives Peace Nobel Prizes to Indians that fit in their Protestant mould of thinking, such as and Mother Teresa, Amartya Sen or Abhijit Banerjee, and neglects real philanthropes, such as Sri Sri Ravi Shankar.

CHAPTER 34

Hindu Power: Its Geostrategic Importance

One rarely hears about India in the western Media, whether newspapers or TV channels, except when there are catastrophes, big elections, or some side stories that often show India in a poor light. Forget about Hindus – most western people, whether they are French or Americans, although they have sympathy for India, often mistake the word 'Indians' with the name 'Hindus' and sometimes, the old confrontation between Christian monotheism and so-called Hindu polytheism crops up in conversations, when it comes to gurus, for instance, whom the French often accuse of creating 'sects'.

Yet, as we saw in the previous chapters, a true Hindu power, holding a series of successive Governments in India, would be secular in nature, as Hinduism has a universal outlook. Hindu kings and queens, such as Shivaji Maharaj, Maharana Pratap, Ahiliabai Holkar, or Krishna Deva Raja of Vijaynagar, were equally lay in their tolerance, never imposing Hinduism as the state religion and respecting the wives and daughters of their enemies.

Soon, the West is going to begin to recognize India's growing economic clout, as is did for China a few decades back. It's already happening a bit, as the Indian GDP overtook for some time the Chinese one, though much remains to be done and the Chinese are performing still doing far better than India in most aspects, including infrastructures, electronic hardware, scientific research and manufacturing. Indeed, the French and the Americans are growing wary of the buying spree of Chinese firms and its government, of western companies, cinemas studios, hotels and castles.... There are an increasing number of Chinese tourists in Paris, New-Yorkor London and they can be seen nowadays in luxury shops, such as Hermes or Dior, where formerly only the Japanese and the Americans bought.

Yet, there is one aspect that western diplomats and governments never think off: it is that an India with a Hindu Power would be of immense geostrategic interest to the West. Why? Firstly, because a Hindu India would be an island of democracy, religious freedom and strength, in an Asia which is racked by Muslim fundamentalism and Chinese threats of hegemony. It is not only Pakistan that exports Islamic terrorism, towards Indian Kashmir and for that matter all over the world, but Afghanistan too, which, as soon as the Americans fully leave, will go back to is old Taliban way and become again a danger to India, Russia and even China. To the East, Indonesia, with the largest Muslim population in the world, can always fall prey to a radical Islamic government, the way Turkey has. A strong Hindu government in Delhi would act as a deterrent to these nations, in Bali for instance, where Hindus are slowly being squeezed out by Muslim colons from Java or mainland Indonesia.

Asia is also the prey of an immense Chinese thirst for military hegemony and gluttony for more territories. China took Tibet, then Honk-Kong, today wants Taiwan, claims that Arunachal Pradesh, a state in eastern India that has borders with Tibet, is its own, is digging deep sea ports in Gwadar (Pakistan), Burma, Sri Lanka – and India finds itself surrounded from all sides: Nepal, where there is a strong Chinese influence; Pakistan, which Beijing has propped-up financially, militarily and even nuclear-wise; Sri Lanka where the Chinese have invested heavily in the last ten years putting the Sri Lankan government in dept; Burma, which likewise owes a lot of money to China, which is much near geographically than Sri Lanka; and in the other extreme, Afghanistan where the Chinese are prospecting minerals. Note here that the West is also falling prey to the nuclear blackmail that Pakistan and China are doing unto them: "if you do not put pressure on India to negotiate Kashmir, the

Pakistanis regularly tell the Americans and Europeans, there will be a nuclear war between us and India, with grave environmental consequences for this Planet." The Chinese have also brought a railroad near the Indian border and built the highest landing strip in the world in Tibet, so that their planes can swoop down on India.

Thus, America has indirectly started using India to counter China's aggressive hold in the Chinese sea and Indian Ocean, particularly regarding the Spratly islands that China has colonized and built a port and an airstrip where its war planes can land, though, it is also claimed by Vietnam, the Philippines and Malaysia. The West is concerned too that the Spratly islands will be used by the Chinese to control the sea-lanes, whereas there should be a free flow of goods and oil for all. India, which has a more powerful navy than Vietnam, Malaysia, or even Japan, is therefore the natural counterweight to China's greediness.

We saw how the successive Indian Governments never could deal in a forceful manner with Chinese duplicity and greed. A strong Hindu Government, would therefore be the perfect buffer for the West to counter Chinese 21st century colonialism. In fact, Modi has already shown this, by allowing the Dalai Lama to visit Arunachal Pradesh, a state, as we saw, that the Chinese claim as its own. And Modi's 2018 visit to Chamoli in Uttarakhand to celebrate Diwali with the troops of the Indo-Tibetan Border Police, also sent the right tough signals to Beijing, something that Washington appreciated. A bolder move would be for India to support a free Tibet movement, which would hurt the Chinese badly, while the Dalai lama is alive – but Narendra Modi may not be ready to do that yet.

In conclusion, the sooner the West will realize that a Hindu India is not only the natural economic alternative to an undemocratic China, but also its legitimate geostrategic ally in Asia, the better for a stable Asia and the future of the world.

CHAPTER 35

The Geostrategic Importance of Tibet

For nearly 70 years, China has humiliated India at every step: It betrayed Nehru's naive trust in a *Hindi-Chini bhai-bhai* friendship and treacherously attacked India from Tibet, which Nehru had implicitly left to the Chinese, beating the Indian army which would take decades to recover. It directly or indirectly encouraged separatist movements in the northeast; it used Nepal as a front state against India; it armed, and worst of all, gave the nuclear bomb to Pakistan, a crime against humanity. Today it is still sitting on a million square meters in Aksai Chin in the Himalayas (supposedly given to Pakistan), which rightfully belong to India; it claims Arunachal Pradesh, and sometimes Sikkim, does regular incursions into Indian territory and is still busy encircling India in Burma. Chinese despise Indians, witness how once they summoned the Indian ambassador in Beijing at 2 am in the morning as if she was some lower hireling.

It is also known that the Chinese think that they can outsmart Indians. Are Indians falling in this trap? It would seem so, witness how the Prime Minister of India, Narendra Modi, went out of his way to woothe Chinese President, Xi Jinping, in Mahabalipuram, rolling the Red Carpet to give him a feel of ancient Indian history and hospitality. But still, China is blocking India's entry in the Nuclear Club and supporting Pakistan terrorists in the United Nations.

Indian leaders, including Narendra Modi, are however perfectly aware that the Chinese, in a span of sixty years, have killed *1,2 million Tibetans*, razed to the ground 6254 monasteries, destroyed 60% of religious, historical and cultural archives and that one Tibetan out of ten is still in jail. As we have entered the Third Millennium, a quarter million Chinese troops are occupying Tibet and there are 7,5 million Chinese settlers for six million Tibetans – in fact, in many places such as the capital, Lhasa, Tibetans are outnumbered two to one....

Seventy years ago, during the Korean war, Sri Aurobindo, had seen clearly in the Chinese game: "the first move in the Chinese Communist plan of campaign is to dominate and take possession first of these northern parts and then of South East Asia as a preliminary to their manoeuvres with regard to the rest of the continent in passing Tibet as a gate opening to India."

And magically, for once, India has a chance to get back at China without appearing to do so. China gives staples visas to Kashmiris and Arunachalis, has also sent soldiers to Pakistan – held Kashmir to protect the New Silk Road that it is building through the Himalaya's, while it suppresses all the freedoms of its own Muslim minority.

So far, India has been helpless in the face of China's cunning duplicity but it has a very powerful weapon that it should use immediately: it would be easy for India to prop-up the Dalai lama, a wonderful man if there is one, and let the Tibetans freely claim their country back, which has never been in Chinese possession except for such short spells. This would embarrass the Chinese enormously and give India some leverage in their territorial negotiations with the Beijing.

Tibet is so important for India: it has always acted as a peaceful, non-violent buffer zone between the two giants of Asia: China and India. And the Dalai-lama wants it even more peaceful: a demilitarized, denuclearized harmony region. But it's exactly the opposite which has happened: according to the CIA, China has transferred one third of its nuclear arsenal to Nagchuka, 250 kms away from Lhasa, a region full of huge caves, which the Chinese have linked together by an intricate underground network and where they have installed nearly one hundred Intercontinental Ballistic Missiles, many of them pointed at Indian cities. The reason for this is that the Chinese, who are probably among the most intelligent people in the world, have always understood that India is their number one potential enemy in Asia – in military, nuclear and economic terms.

If there is one thing that rattles the Chinese and makes them lose their cool, it is the Dalai Lama, the very name 'Dalai Lama' is enough for the Chinese Government to Levy all kinds of threats which are all unpractical. And yet, the Dalai Lama is such a wonderful being, a friend of India, a man that holds no ill – will towards anybody, including the Chinese; a man that has prayed and meditated all his life and ceaselessly travelled the world to preach the Tibetan Cause, a saint, and avatar maybe.... But when the Dalai Lama dies – and he is 85 already, the Chinese will immediately nominate their own Dalai Lama, as they did for the Pancha Karma. So far, His Holiness has refused to say that he will reincarnate himself, as it has been the tradition for centuries. He even said that the next Dalai Lama maybe elected or that it could be a woman.... I am aghast that the Indian Government is oblivious of the fact that the future, freedom and continuity of Tibet is essential not only for India's future but also for the World. A war between India and China, even if it is only conventional, is very probable: China keeps taunting India by making incursions in Ladakh or Sikkim and every time Indian and Chinese troops face each other in tense and encounters. In case of a full – fledged- war China possesses an immense strategic advantage because it can swoop down to India from Tibet like it did in 1962. For the world, the disappearing of the Tibetan spirituality, love and compassion would be an irreparable loss.

Yet India always bends backwards to please the Chinese. Why is that so? Because the Indian intelligentsia, the «secular» politicians, the journalists, the top bureaucrats, are the descendants of these « Brown Shahibs », which Macaulay created more than 250 years ago. The man who thought that « all the historical information which can be collected from all the books which have been written in the Sanskrit language, is less valuable than what may be found in the most paltry abridgement used at preparatory schools in England », wished to make of Indians a darker version of the British. He has been immensely successful and has created a nation with a colonized mind. Many of India's politicians, bureaucrats and journalists, has we repeatedly emphasized, are always aping whatever the West does, or are always worrying about what the West thinks of them. They never think Indian, they have no idea about India's great culture, philosophy and spirituality. Very few have read the Bhagavad Gita, or understood that it encourages yoga in action and that sometimes it is important to defend one's country, culture and borders, by force if necessary. They are no match for Chinese, who are proud of themselves and their nation and will use any means, open and covert, legal and foul, to foster their dream of a Greater China.

CHAPTER 36

The Secret Brotherhood of Hindus and Jews

For 40 years, India did not have relations with Israel. Yet, India and Israel share so much in common and both can learn a lot from each other! Hindus and Jews, far from being the persecutors of minorities, that the Marxist, Arab and INC lobby like to portray, have been persecuted for nearly two thousand years and have been the victims of the two worst genocides in the sad history of humanity: Hitler, in his monstrous quest for a "pure" Aryan race, murdered six millions Jews in his gas chambers during the Second World War; and Belgium historian Koenraad Elst estimates that between the year 1000 and 1525, eighty million Hindus died at the hands of Muslim invaders, probably the biggest holocaust in the whole history of our planet.

Indians and Israelis of today also share in common an awesome problem with Muslim fundamentalists. And India should learn a lesson of two from the way Israel handles this problem, however much it is criticized by the western medias. Unlike India, which since Independence has chosen to deal with this problem in the Gandhian spirit, that is by compromising most of the time with Islamic intransigence – if not giving in (except recently in Kashmir bu abrogating at last Article 370) – Israel showed that toughness first, accompanied later by negotiations pays much more. Basically, the "land for money" concept is something that India should learn from: in 1967, Israel was threatened to be engulfed by its fanatic neighbors, so it stole the initiative by crushing them in a lightning six days war and kept some land which it used later as bargaining chips with Egypt and Syria. India is also surrounded by hostile Muslim countries: Pakistan, Afghanistan, and more and more Bangladesh. So far, India has followed the Nehruvian policy of Good Neighborhood: you give first, expecting that your neighborhood will reciprocate the gesture later. Unfortunately, history has shown that India mostly gets stabbed in the back for its generosity by small insignificant nations such as Bangladesh, which owes its freedom to the sacrifices of India's soldiers and is more and more lending its territory to the ISI. If during the 1965 Indo-Pak war, India would have kept a chunk of the Pakistani territory it has conquered, or if during the Kargil war, it had carried on with its victorious momentum by seizing some of the Pakistan-held Kashmir, which could be used as a buffer zone, there would be probably today less cross-border terrorism.

There is another area where India has a lot to learn from Israel, it is the VVIP security. We all know how it has become here a status symbol, a constant hassle for the ordinary citizen, who has to wait endlessly in his car for the VVIP motorcade to pass by, or in his plane for the Prime Minister of India to land. Sonia Gandhi must have been the most protected leader in the world – and it was a very heavy-handed, unfriendly and ultimately inefficient protection, which is not really warranted, as she is a friend of the Muslims and the Marxists. But look at the Israelis: their Prime Minister moves around with only a few boyish looking men, in sneakers and civil dress and they don't rough up onlookers or hassle innocent citizens. As for potential hijacks of Indian planes, again we have to look towards Israel, whose airline, EL Al, is the safest in the world, in spite of being the most threatened. But for them, no rude cops who hardly talk any English frisking you at airports, but civil and educated EL Al employees, who ask polite but pointed questions and unobtrusive security in the airports and aboard their aircrafts. Israelis have also shown that you should NEVER give in to terrorist demands and also that its commandos are the best. 24 years ago, when an Air France airplane, carrying mostly Israelis, was hijacked by Arab terrorists and forced to land in faraway Uganda, which like the Taliban, in the case of the Indian Airline hijack under Vajpayee, were actually protecting the terrorists while pretending to help in the release of the passengers, Israel in one of the most daring rescue operation ever, sent its commandos flying in the dead of the night over half of the world, killed the terrorists, freed the passengers and brought them back to Israel with very little casualties. Unfortunately, India adopted a total opposite attitude during the hijack of IC 814, with the catastrophic result that we know: the terrorists released are today openly preaching in Pakistan a jihad unto death towards India.

There is also another aspect from which India can learn a great deal from Israel and it is its language. In 1948, Israel regained part of it Holy land and Israelis, who had been scattered all over the world, came back to live in Israel. There was one problem though: they all spoke different languages and no tongue unified them except Yiddish, a bastard language spoken by the Jews of Eastern Europe. So, the state of Israel set its scholars to revive Hebrew, Israel's ancient language, which had fallen in decrepitude, so that today everybody speaks Hebrew and it has unified Israel like nothing else. India should invite some of these linguists and they should sit down with Sanskrit scholars and devise a way of simplifying and modernizing Sanskrit, which is the mother of all European tongues, a language so subtle and rich that it will energize and revitalize the whole Indian culture.

And finally, Like Indians, Israel is one of those 'elected people of God', of whom Sri Aurobindo speaks in his book the "Hour of God", who have managed to keep their spirituality alive in spite of oppressions, invasions and genocides. That the Israelis turned their back on their avatar and crucified him, may account for their sufferings for two thousand years, as India went through these centuries of atoning for its 'black karma'. But both, in their own ways, are becoming again powerful nations, vibrant with spirituality and vigor.

CHAPTER 37

Does Hindu Power Need a War to Really Emerge: The Hindu Power Kurukshetra War of the 21st Century

« There is nothing wrong about war", once said Sri Aurobindo. And it is true that throughout the ages, war has been an essential part of man's life on this planet and there have been very few periods in modern history which have not seen strife. The French fought three bloody wars against the Germans in the last 125 years, India has battled five wars in 55 years, four against Pakistan, if you count Kargil, and one against the Chinese.

Of course, the horrors of war, the devastation it creates, have been documented enough so that there is no need to delve upon them. In the olden times, it was accepted as a fact of life and very few people protested. Actually, of all the nations in the world, India is the one who handled best the business of war, as Sri Aurobindo points out: "Vedic India allowed for men's inclination to war, but made sure that it never went beyond a certain stage, for only professional armies fought and the majority of the population remained untouched." Indeed, at no time in ancient India, were there great fratricidal wars, like those between the British and the French, or even the Protestants and the Catholics within France itself.

But today, as there is a new awareness of the value of life, both human, animal and vegetal, man often recoils from the terrors of conflicts and its consequences on the human being and its environment. Naturally also, humanity aspires to a more harmonious life, where not only will it not be necessary to kill each other to survive, but also where all human beings would love and respect each other, regardless of their colour, religion and nationality. Thus, particularly in the United States during the Vietnam war, there manifested amongst the youth this longing for "no war, but peace," as symbolized by the famous photo of a young American girl sticking a flower in the barrel of the gun of a national Guard. This anti-war pressure was so great that it took out the wind of the Unites States to fight this bloody conflict in a faraway country. and ultimately it surrendered meekly Vietnam to the Vietcongs. Since then, although there is no more such anti-war movement in the United States, American soldiers seem to have lost their valour and now their wars are fought from the safety of supersonic planes and very rarely on the ground. And as soon as a few American, or French, or English soldiers are killed, the will to fight goes, because of intense media and public pressure on Governments. This is why hijackers and kidnappers have such a field day now: they kill one or two people and whole governments surrender, as seen during the hijack of the Kathmandu-Delhi flight in December 1999. It takes Israelis soldiers to keep on fighting with their own public, press and government behind them, when suicide after suicide bombers kill scores of innocent people every month.

In India too, there has risen a strong, coherent anti-war lobby. Intellectuals such as Arundhadi Roy have brilliantly pleaded for a peaceful and restrained India, powerful but benevolent, who learns not to retaliate, to be merciful and generous towards her smaller neighbours. The spectre of a nuclear war has of course come as a strong argument for the anti-war lobby in India and we have seen in the last two weeks how both foreign correspondents and Indian magazines have used the available data on the horrendous consequences of a nuclear war to put pressure on the Government to back out from a conflict with Pakistan.

At any rate, Indian Governments have not been exceptionally bold militarily. Two factors appear to have inhibited the Indian courage to face adversity when faced with threats: the first is

Buddhism, which made out of non-violence a rigid creed; and the second is the Mahatma Gandhi's equally unbending theorem of non-violence, which may have precipitated India's partition. And this is why maybe, under the guise of non-violence and peace, so many Indian intellectuals and politicians have shied away from war since independence, witness Nehru's refusal to heed warnings about China's hostility, which triggered the humiliation of the Indian army in 1962.

But will there be a nuclear war? Pakistan, whatever its obsession about Kashmir, which is basically a revenge for the loss of Eastern Pakistan, now Bangladesh, thanks to India's support, is ruled by intelligent men: they know that if they do manage to drop one nuclear bomb on Delhi or Bombay, there will no more Pakistan worth the name, as all major Pakistani cities will be wiped off the face of the earth. Islam, who has made of the use of violence a near religious practice, understands the language of violence: see how it kept quiet when America showed its muscle after the 11th September attack, or when the Allies invaded Iraq. Thus, the Pakistani government is doing a nuclear blackmail on the world... which is unfortunately working, as so many nations keep putting so much pressure on India to negotiate Kashmir.

If there is a war between Pakistan and India, whatever the politicians say, it will be a war between two brothers, for except for their religion, everything unite Indians and Pakistanis: their colour, ethnic origin, food habits, language... In fact, some Indian Muslim soldiers might have to shoot on some Pakistani cousins, or uncles. Will they pull the trigger when their commander says so? Will not their conscience tell them that it is wrong to shoot on one's brothers? Does not that remind you of something? Did not Arjuna face the same dilemma five thousand years ago in Kurukshetra? Did he not throw his bow on the ground and tell Krishna: "no I will not fight, because war is such a horrible thing and I refuse to kill my bothers."

But what does Krishna tell him: "not only you are not killing the soul, but merely the material body; but also, sometimes, when all other means have failed and it is necessary to protect one's borders, wives, children and culture, war can become *dharma*. And that brings in the final question: is a war against Pakistan justified? Would it be *dharma*? Well you have to decide for yourself: for nearly forty years Pakistan has waged a proxy war against India in Punjab, in Kashmir and now more and more in the North-East; it has killed thousands of innocent people, raped women dismembered children, mutilated Indian soldiers in the most horrible manner... Several Indian Prime Ministers have made one-sided attempts at peace, without getting reciprocity from Islamabad.

Indeed, a war between Pakistan and India might be the Kurukshestra of the 21st century, the ultimate war which will set right fifteen hundred years of Islamic terror and both redeem the Hindus' karma of cowardice, as well as the Muslims' karma of bloodshed. This war, if it ever happens, will also pave the way for the reunification of India and Pakistan, by force or by natural means. For the two brothers can fight for a time, but ultimately, they have to embrace each other anew, as they are basically one, beyond time and body, as Krishna once told Arjuna.

Chapter 38

What is True Hindu-ness?

A country needs a people who are proud of their own culture and civilisation to move forward. That is what true nationalism – not jingoism – is about. It also requires an intelligentsia which reflects this pride in its newspapers, books, paintings, sculpture, sports even. But for this purpose, both intellectuals and grassroot people have to be groomed in the intricacy, the subtlety and genius of their own culture, while not being blind to its faults. We have thus to educate the children of India and this is why this book is addressed to all Indian youth, specially the Hindus, wherever they are from, from whichever strata of Indian society they originate, whatever is their first language. It will endeavour to teach them why it is a great privilege to be born an Hindu today and what travails, pitfalls and genocides, their culture had to endure throughout the centuries. Then only will each Indian askhimself this question:" what can I do for my country"? "In what way can I contribute to this great nation which is India"?

What is it to be an Indian today? What is meant by Indian-ness, this natural inner space, which automatically confers certain qualities?

Firstly, and foremost: "I accept you; I accept that you may be White or Black, Red or Yellow, Christian, Buddhist, or Muslim." Not only that, "but I am even ready to go and worship in a church or a mosque, besides my temple." "I accept that my Gods are avatars, incarnations of the Divine, but so are Jesus Christ, and also Buddha and even Mohamed." This is why India has always been a country of freedom, where all persecuted religious minorities in the world have found refuge over the centuries, whether the Jews, the Parsis, the Syrian Christians, or today the Tibetans.

This accepting of the other is an extraordinary statement and a marvellous instrument towards world peace, at a time when the two great monotheist religions of the world, Islam and Christianity, still say: "there is only one true God in the world – mine – and if you worship any other god, you are an Infidel and a Pagan and it is my right to convert you by any means, or even to kill you." The 11th September 2001 attacks are nothing but a consequence of that dangerous theorem.

What else? "I have inherited from my ancestors the tools to become a better man, whatever my religion, ethnicity and profession: a better Christian, a better Hindu, a better Muslim, a better carpenter, or CEO, IT engineer, or sailor." What are these tools? Hata-yoga, India's gift to the world, which has been copied and imitated everywhere (although Time magazine did a story on yoga without mentioning the name "India" once). What else? Meditation, this extraordinary technique of coming back to one's Self, of settling the mind and the body, which is today practiced by millions around the world – another bequest of India to humanity. Pranayama, the science of respiration, perfected by Indians for three millenniums. "Does the breath have any religion," asks Sri Sri Ravi Shankar, the founder of the Art of Living movement, which has spread today in 140 countries?

Obviously, the West is not only fast food, artificial lights, cars and a superficial vitality. There is certain openness, for instance, about America, a willingness of the American people to listen to other points of view, which is unique. Yes, America is also a land of freedom where in the last three hundred years, people from all nationalities, all social classes, have been given the chance to make it good - the fact that it elected Obama, a black leader, shows it. And they have in turn responded to this unique trust by giving the United States their 100% allegiance and energies, which makes it today the leading industrial and military nation in the world. One finds too a sense of collectiveness, a caring for the others, which gives America some of the best road system in the world and first-class public amenities, like the community centers found in many American cities.

But is America really a benevolent, casteless society? Well, for one, what the White Americans, for instance, did to the Blacks not that long ago, must be ranking amongst some of the saddest deeds perpetuated by one class of humanity on another; not to speak of the terrible and shameful treatment inflicted upon the hapless Red Indians, the original inhabitants of their land. There are also a lot of inequalities in the States: extremely rich people and some incredibly poor folks. American journalists and human rights activists like to highlight the "oppressed" condition of women in India. But as early as the late sixties, India elected democratically a woman Prime Minister, the highest post of the nation – and that for nearly twenty years. Can the country of triumphant feminism and gender equality boast of a woman President – Hillary Clinton did not make it this time at least? The problem is that most Indians suffer too much from an inferiority complex vis à vis the West, to point this out to the Americans who are constantly criticizing India for its human rights in Kashmir and Gujarat.

Yes, in America one enjoys the liberty to do whatever one wants without the red tape, bureaucracy and heavy taxation that one is subjected to in India, or even in industrialized countries such as France. But after 11th September 2001, freedoms have been heavily curtailed in the US, especially if you have a brown skin, as many Indians, are finding out today, being mistaken by ignorant Americans for Pakistanis, Afghanis or Saudis. Today, each of your movements is watched in the US, as there are video cameras everywhere, not only at airports, but also at traffic lights, in stores, at cinemas. Everything is known about you, thanks to computerization – and we even once heard on the PA of Atlanta airport: "you can go to jail for something you say as a joke!" Compare this to India: I have lived here for 50 years, I have gone to the most remote places, traveled to sacred spots with my cameras, tape recorder and white face. And never once have I been aggressed, never once has my passport been asked in the streets (try traveling in the subway in Paris if you have a brown face and a leather jacket), never once have I been mugged at late nights in Delhi, Mumbai or Chennai, whereas in Washington, the capital of the 'land of freedom', we were told not to go out alone in certain parts after 8 PM.

Many people speak about the extraordinary "religious freedom one can enjoy in the US, where nobody bothers whether you are a Jew, a Hindu, or a Christian." Fair enough. But let's put it that way: the American population is overwhelmingly Christian and nobody there finds anything to say that the President of the United States is sworn in on the Bible, or that in some states a Christian prayer is uttered before the start of the school. India has a thumping Hindu majority (80%), but imagine the uproar if Modi was sworn in on the Bhagavad-Gita! Yet, India had three Muslim Presidents since independence. Did the US ever have a Muslim President?

Would it be good if all Indians settled in the US should regroup themselves under a "Hindu American banner," it does look as if I want to exclude Christians, Muslim and Sikh Indians. But the question is: do these minorities really want to be part of India? Let's answer the objections from Christians first. One Christian reader tells me "Christians have no freedom in India and that from time to time churches have been attacked. But these are very isolated cases and our friend disregards what the Christians have done to Hindus over the centuries. The first Christian community in the world, that of the Syrian Christians, settled in India in the first century. They were not only allowed to practice their religion in peace, but they prospered here, whereas at the same time they were persecuted in Rome and later in many Arabic countries. But when Vasco de Gama landed in India in the 16th century, the Portuguese, with the active collaboration of many of the Indian Christians, unleashed a reign of terror in Goa and some parts of Kerala, crucifying Brahmins, razing temples, forcibly marrying their soldiers to Goanese women. The British, even if they did not use such violent means, gave a free hand to missionaries to convert huge parts of India, particularly in the North-East. Today, American or Australian dollars are used to still convert unethically, by using the economic incentive amongst tribals and untouchables, teaching the new converts to hate their culture and customs and creating a spirit of separatism, as the Christian Bodo and Mizo militants have shown.

A few Sikh friends also resented my not having mentioned Sikkism. Let me quote straightaway from Sri Aurobindo: "The Sikh Khalsa was an astonishingly original and novel creation and its face was turned not to the past but to the future. Apart and singular in its theocratic head and democratic soul and structure, it was the first attempt to combine the deepest elements of Islam and Vedanta. But it could not create between the spirit and the external life the transmitting medium of a rich creative thought and culture. And thus, hampered and deficient it began and ended with narrow local limits, achieved intensity but no power of expansion..."

Unfortunately, the Sikhs, because they had to defend themselves against the terrible persecutions by the Muslims, became a militant religion, adopting hawkish habits, which they kept, even in time of peace. And they also retained some of the more negative sides of Islam: intolerance, or feeling of persecution, thus cutting themselves from the mainstream spirit of Hindu tolerance from which they anyway came, and where they might ultimately go back. But do they not come from the great Hindu family? Has not till lately every good Hindu family donated one of their sons to Sikhism? Do not Hindus, still today go to Gurdwaras? Yet today, many expatriate Sikhs want to have nothing to do with Hinduism, and sometimes even with India. Badrinath, a holy place to Hindus and Hemkunt Saheb, the most important place of pilgrimage for Sikhs after the Golden Temple, are only separated by a few kilometers. You will find Hindus taking the very arduous trek up to Hemkunt Saheb, but today hardly any Sikhs bother to take the bus to Badrinath. By cutting itself from its roots, Sikhism might be running adrift and lose its relevance.

What about Indian Muslims? Today we see, even though they benefit in India from a freedom they would not have in Saudi Arabia, or even in Pakistan, that Indian Muslims often feel their first allegiance goes to Islam and not to India. The irony of it all is that Muslims invaded India, raped it repeatedly, ran it with an iron and bloody hand, attempted to make of India a totally Islamic country by forcibly converting millions of Hindus – and today they manage to portray themselves in the eyes of the world as the persecuted! When fed-up by centuries of Muslim oppression, persecutions, ostracism and separatism, upper caste, as well as lower caste Hindus in Gujarat burst out in a frenzy of unforgivable violence after the burning of 57 innocent Hindus in a train by a Muslim mob, Indian Muslims cry for revenge: "I invite people to commit crimes against Hindus in Gujarat," said one of the emails from a Muslim gentleman. Another Muslim lady, Shabnam Hashmi, has been going around all the United-States, saying that it was the RSS who killed the hapless kar sevaks in the Sabamarti Express – and she got the ear of all US mainstream newspapers, such as the NYT, as well as many Government-backed human right agencies. Are American that stupid to believe such a terrible lie? Isn't it time that the Indian Muslim community, both abroad and in India, most of whom are Hindus who had to convert by force, make a choice between Babar, a man who destroyed everything which was good, beautiful and holy and lived by the power of violence and Ram, who believed in the equality of all and gave-up all riches and honors of the world because he thought his bother deserved the throne more than him?

Another strong objection from some readers: religion divides. First let me say that Hinduism, as Sri Aurobindo or Vivekananda, or Shri Ramakrishna envisioned it, is not a religion but a living spirituality which has given to the world - and still gives it today – wonderful tools: hata-yoga copied all over this planet, meditation, or pranayama, which, says Sri Sri Ravi Shankar "can be practiced by anybody, whatever their nationality and religion." Secondly, at a time when the two largest monotheistic religions of the world, Islam and Christianity still claim that their God is the only true one and it is still their right in the 21st century to convert, or even kill in the name of Jesus Christ, or Mohamed, Hindus, through the extraordinary concept of the avatar, recognize that God manifests himself at different times, in different countries, under different names and thus grant to everybody the right to worship God under any form. This is a very precious spiritual (and not religious) knowledge which has been lost to the world and which, even the humblest Hindu peasant spontaneously practices.

It is also true that things in India are not as they should be. Hindus there are not united, India is divided along caste and religious lines by unscrupulous politicians. Yes, Hindus can also be racists, they do suffer at the same time, as someone commented, from a big inferiority complex, as well as one of superiority, quite an achievement! Yes, it is as well correct that expatriate Indians do often tend to become more conscious of their roots than India Indians: they will send their children to learn Bharata Natyam and will remember all the festivals. Good: there is a whole generation of upper middle-class kids in India who are so desperately aping the worst of the West, that they are lost for India. Yes, Hindus can on top pf that be selfish, passive, cowardly, miserly, whereas many of them are extremely rich. But nevertheless, they remain a wonderful people, alive with an inbred joy and spirituality.

Contrary to what some assert, there is a definite atmosphere in India, something special, something unique, which is there nowhere else in the world. Those of you who spent a lot of time abroad, will notice a certain quality in the atmosphere as soon as you enter India, if you are a little sensitive. There is nothing miraculous about it, it juts springs from millions of sages, yogis, thinkers, sadhus, avatars having incarnated themselves on this sacred land of India and meditated there and preached love and compassion. This can be felt even more strongly at certain locations: on the banks of Benares, in Rishikesh or Haridwar, in Madurai, or even of all the places, in Srinagar, where there is still today a strong spiritual atmosphere, maybe because it was once the cradle of Shivaism.

So: Indian Americans or Hindu Americans? To start with, there are already Indian Americans, those that Columbus mistook for real Indians and you can't usurp their names. Secondly it ultimately depends on the Christians, the Sikhs and the Muslims, who in the last few decades, have drifted more and more from the Indian psyche, striving to strike a fundamental identity of their own. India and Hinduism always gave them space to express themselves and left them the full freedom of religious expression. But in return, Muslims and Christians persecuted the Hindus; and Sikhs, let themselves be used by Pakistan to harm India's collective unity. We have also seen that the numerous Indian Americans associations in the US, where there are indeed Muslim, Christians and Sikh Indians, are frequently paralyzed by these three groups, who although they are very small in numbers, often work against India and the Hindu majority by creating such forums as the South Asian journalist Association, which is sometimes used as an anti-Hindu/India forum by Pakistanis, Bangladeshis and Indian Muslims.

Thus, if Hindus in the United States, Canada, England or Australia regroup themselves under a "Hindu American" label it might prompt the three minorities to wake-up to the reality of a stronger, overwhelmingly Hindu majority. On top of that, as I have already said, it will give a clear-cut identity to Hindus abroad, dissociating them from the Pakistanis, the Bangladeshis, the Saudis, or the Afghans, who have a much less friendly attitude towards the West than Hindus. It will also help make known to the average Westerner the extraordinary achievements of the Hindu community abroad, which must be the most upwardly mobile – and perhaps the richest – community in the West. Lastly, it will help the Indian Government, by creating a powerful and effective lobby in the US, Canada, England or Australia free from the shackles imposed by the Christian, Sikh and Muslim Indians. Ultimately, it will up to these three minorities to decide whether they want to re-join this great family that is "Induism". For we should then give back to 'Hindus' it proper meaning: Indus from the civilization of the valley of Indus, probably the most ancient civilization of the world still active today. Once upon a time, Indian Christians, Parsis, Muslims and Hindus were called 'Indus' by the invaders without differentiation of caste and religion. Is it not time to put back this habit into practice?

CHAPTER 39

Ten Challenges for Hindus in the 21st Century

Let us say again: every 6th person on this Planet is a Hindu and Hindus still constitute the overwhelming majority in India – nearly 80% of the population. Humanity needs thus to re-discover the wonder that is Hinduism, the oldest spirituality still in practice in the world. It is also true that Hindus must to rise to the challenges of this second millennium. Here they are – in order of difficulty.

1. Break the Polytheist image. One of the most enduring clichés about Hinduism is that Hindus adore a multitude of gods and goddesses, which makes them heathens in the eyes of Christians, thus good to be converted to the 'true' God, often with unethical financial baits; and 'kafirs' for Muslims from all over the world, particularly from neighbouring countries, such as Pakistan, which encourages them to wage a jihad on India.

Yet, Hinduism, whether you want to call it a religion or a spiritual system, is without doubt one of the most monotheist creeds in the world, because it always recognized *that the One is Many and that He incarnates Himself or Herself in a multitude of forms – hence the million of gods and goddesses in the Hindu pantheon*. Vedic Sages (from the Vedas, the oldest and most sacred Scriptures of Hinduism) had understood that man has to be given a multiplicity of different approaches to the Unfathomable. And truly, for the Hindus, the Divine cannot be "this" or "that" – *neti, neti*. In its essence, He cannot be several - or even one – and thus can never be perfectly seized by the human mind. Indeed, Hindus, who were once upon a time the best dialecticians in the world (and this is maybe why they are today the top software programmers of this planet), were able to come-up with this kind of equation: (a) God is in the world; (b) the world is in God; (c) the world is God; (d) God and the world are distinct; (e) God is distinct from the world, but the world is not distinct from God; (f) it is impossible to discern if the world is distinct from God or not.... Never has the unique nature of Hindu polytheism been better defined.

Hindus in the world need to emphasize to their western brothers and sisters that they have also always recognized the divinity of other religions, as their concept of the *avatar* (the different forms that the Divine takes at different times to incarnate Himself or Herself in a human form) helped them to accept the reality of other prophets, masters or gurus. It is, for instance, perfectly acceptable for an ordinary Hindu to have on his wall the image of Krishna, alongside the one of Buddha, one of the Christ, with a few photos of the Mecca or even John Fitzgerald Kennedy! And Hindus have always worshipped at non-Hindu places, such as Velangani, the Christian seat of pilgrimage of South India, or some Sufi shrine in Kashmir or Rajasthan. It should be said too that Hindus *never* tried to convert others to their own religion, not even by peaceful means, as the Buddhists did all over Asia; and their armies never but oh, never, set to conquer other nations to impose their own culture and religion, as Islam and Christianity did, often in a bloody manner. Thus, Hindus in the WORLD, need to be able to counter in a knowledgeable manner, verbally or in writing (letters to editors, etc.) this wrong polytheist image which has harmed them.

2. Dispel the image of poverty attached to India. One of the reasons Hindus are not taken too seriously abroad, is that their country, India, is always associated with poverty. True, there is still poverty in India, social inequality, but since 1947, thanks to the Green Revolution, there has been no famine. Hindus in the world and in India can always counter this pervading untruth in the mind of the westerners, by stating that according to British records, one million Indians died of famine between 1800 and 1825; 4 million between

1825 and 1850; 5 million between 1850 and 1875; and *15 million* between 1875 and 1900. Thus, 25 million Indians died in one hundred years under the benevolent rule of the British Raj!

Poverty in India is also commercially exploited by Hollywood and writers. A book such as 'The City of Joy', by Frenchman Dominique Lapierre, which was a huge success worldwide, gives the impression that India is a vast slum, which is absolutely untrue – and the author, who often comes to India, had to know that he was inducing his readers in error. As for the film "Slumdog Millionnaire", which raked-up so many Oscars, it is even more perverse: it says things which are false, portrays situations that are untrue, such as the young boy throwing himself in excrements, to get an autograph of India's film star Amitabh Bacchan and should have been boycotted by Hindus.

Yet, India is a **wealthy** country. It is said, even today, because of the socialist policies of previous governments and the heavy taxation, that half of India's money is in the black. The poverty is only there because of the mismanagement, the dishonesty, and the inheritance of wrong structures. For Indians must be with some of the best savers in the world. And they don't hoard in abstract concepts: they go in for solid gold, land, cash – and that from the little shopkeeper to the business magnate.

As economic liberalisation is happening in India at this very moment, the rise of India as a superpower will herald the rise of the status of Hindus in the US, UK, Canada and all over the world, for today the assessment that every industrial nation in the world casts on another country, is primarily economical. Thus China is respected so much today in the world, not for its political power, which is overshadowed by immense Human Rights abuses (Mao Tse Tung killed 3 million of his own people during the Cultural revolution and it has been calculated that one million Tibetans have been murdered by the Chinese), but by its economic clout. In the same way, India's image, whose PIB has now overtaken China's, will shed many of the prejudices attached to her, when the world takes notice of the huge investment possibilities there.

3. Explain the caste system to westerners. Caste is still a curse that hangs around India's neck. While it is true that 75% marriages are still arranged in India, Hindus in the US, UK, Canada and elsewhere need to whisper in the ears of their western friends that the Indian Government has made tremendous efforts since 1947 to uplift the lower castes. And it has succeeded in great measure. Tell them that your present Prime Minister comes from one of the lowest castes and was a tea seller, that some of today's Indian Chief Ministers are untouchables, or that one of India's best known saints, Amrita Anandamayi, who has hundreds of thousands of disciples in the WORLD, and millions all over the world, and has built hospitals, universities, housings for the poor, comes from the lowest caste possible in Kerala.

You can also ask your US and European friends if the caste system is really that worse than the huge class differences you can see nowadays in Europe or the USA!

4. Dispel the notion that Hindus can be fundamentalists and violent. Hindus need to repeat again and again to their Western brothers and sisters that the only country in the world where Jews were never persecuted is India. Tell them that the genius of this country lies in its Hindu ethos, or rather in the true spirituality behind Hinduism. Explain that the average Hindu that you meet in a million villages, possesses this simple, innate spirituality in his or her genes and accepts your diversity, whether you are Christian, Muslim, or Jain, Arab, French or Chinese. It is this 'Hindu-ness' (which cannot be experienced if you sit in Delhi most of the time) that makes most Indian Christians different, from say a French Christian, or an Indian Muslim unlike a Saudi Muslim. Also that Hindus have given refuge to all persecuted minorities of the world, whether the Syrian Christians, the Parsis (Iranian worshippers of Zarathustra), the Jews, the Armenians, or today the Tibetans (the real Tibet is in India now, as the one in the hands of the Chinese has lost much of its Tibetan character). Thus you cannot find *less* fundamentalist than a Hindu in this world and Hindus in the world should immediately react when they read articles in the western Press (often unfortunately from New Delhi-based correspondents) trying to equate Islamic terrorism, which blow-up innocent civilians, to angry ordinary Hindus who burn churches without killing anybody. Tell them that however reprehensible was the destruction of the Babri Masjid (a Mosque built in the 15th century by Muslim invader Babar on a very ancient and holy Hindu temple dedicated to the God Ram), no Muslim was killed in the process; compare this with the 'vengeance' bombings of 1993 in Mumbai, which wiped-out hundreds of innocent, mostly Hindus. Yet, the Babri Masjid destruction is often described by journalists as the most horrible act of the two. Today, you can argue with your Western friends, Hindus are one of the most successful, law abiding and integrated communities in the world. Can you call them terrorists?

5. Tell your western friends about the greatness of Hindu philosophy and Literature. Indian education is a leftover from the British Raj. Nothing wrong with that, except that as a result, Indian students know all about Shakespeare, Napoleon, the Bible, but very little about their great warriors. And there were many: Shivaji Maharaj from Maharashtra, as great as a warrior as Napoleon, who started the first Indian navy, made laws, protected women and children from all religions; Maharana Pratap from Rajasthan, the only Rajput (maharaja, if you wish) who stood up to the Moghol invaders in the 17th century); and even great women warriors, the equals of Jeanne d'Arc: the Rani of Jhansi, who fought the British; Ahilyabai of Indore, who had the first women battalion in India, or Chennama in the South. Tell you Western friends that some of the greatest poets who walked on this earth were Hindus: Kalidasa, whose Sanskrit was so pure, than even translated in English it still shines; Vyasa, who composed the Mahabharata, which has been considered by many western authors, of the same epic quality of the Iliad and Odyssey, etc.

Western philosophy and culture trace its sources to ancient Greece.... But many famous writers and Indologists have pointed out that Greece was greatly influenced by Hinduism. Famous Indianist

Jean Herbert reminds us that "many many centuries before us, India had devised most of the philosophical systems which Europe experienced with later. They contained, at least in its essence, the philosophy of the Greeks, the Alexandrine mystique, the religious speculation of the Middle Ages, the rationalism of the XIXth century and even the most recent incarnations of modern pantheism." In 1782, already, French philosopher Pierre Sonnerat had written: "Ancient India gave to the world its religions and philosophies: Egypt and Greece owe India their wisdom and it is known that Pythagoras went to India to study under Brahmins, who were the most enlightened of human beings."

But it is in XIXth century Europe that an open admiration for ancient India's culture flourished best, particularly in Germany, where philosophers, such a Frederich Shlegel, said that "there is no language in the world, even Greek, which has the clarity and the philosophical precision of Sanskrit," adding "that India is not only at the origin of everything, she is superior in everything, intellectually, religiously or politically – and even the Greek heritage seems pale in comparison..." The great Shopenhauer agrees with him and writes in the preface of his "*The World as a Will and as a Representation:*" "According to me, the influence of Sanskrit literature on our time will not be lesser than what was in the XVIth century Greece's influence on Renaissance. One day, India's wisdom will flow again on Europe and will totally transform our knowledge and thought." And Nietzsche himself had read the Vedas, which he admired profoundly, could quote from the Law of Manu and thought that "Buddhism and Brahmanism are a hundred times deeper and more objective than Christianity."

6. Hindus in the world should preserve their Indian-ness. As we have seen above, Hindus in the US or Britain, or elsewhere, have to ask themselves that question: what is it to be an Indian abroad today? What is meant by Indian-ness ? How much of yourself do you give to your Western identity – and how much space do you preserve for your Indian-ness ? For we see many of the children of Indians who settled in the world twenty or thirty years ago, merge themselves totally in the British way of life, speak with an English accent, eat fish fry, support Chelsea football club ... and in the process forget all about their wonderful Indian culture....

What second, third or even fourth generations Hindus in the West should also ask themselves today is "How can I repay my debt to India?" After all not only they got a nearly free education in India which was good enough for them to obtain well paid jobs in the US, UK, or elsewhere in the West, but did they not also inherit that certain Indian-ness, which has been a great help to adapt to the western way of life. Or: "In what way can I contribute to this great nation which is India, which is often maligned and side-lined in the US and Europe?" It would be a blow to both Britain (or the US or Canada, or France) if Hindus would totally blend in their countries of adoption and lose their values of tolerance, gentleness, hospitality and the ability to see the One in the Many, it would be not only a loss to themselves, but also to their countries of adoption, to which they would not bring anything special.

7. Take political power and Unite. You know by now that wherever Hindus exiled themselves, they did well, whether as labourers in Mauritius or doctors in the WORLD or IT engineers in the USA! They pay their taxes, integrate themselves, do not riot, their children top in colleges and universities and generally blend in the culture of the country they adopted. Everybody also knows that some of the biggest multinationals, such as Adobe, Microsoft, Diageo, Mastercard, Google, Pepsi, or others are today headed by Indians – read Hindus.

Yet, Hindus are individualistic people and they tend to look down on politics, as something 'dirty'. This is why they did not always get the politicians they deserve in their home country. We see today that a lot of Muslims are elected in local boroughs or even towns in the US, UK or Canada. That is good and should be praised. But it is also true that often these Muslim leaders tend to think only of their community and sometimes use their offices to enforce the vision of their particular communities, such as segregated swimming pools, or even try to modify western textbooks. Hindus, with their universal outlook will not do such things. But they need to come out of their shells and stand for elections at all levels of the US, British and Canada political system.

Another drawback of Hindus in the West, particularly in the USA, is that they are terribly disunited and are splintered in many groups, along states of origins, profession, or even castes, sometimes even are at odds with each other. Hindus in West should therefore unite under one umbrella organization and the united Hindu diaspora leadership should meet at least once a year with a rotating president.

8. **Explain Narendra Modi**. As Modi is well in a second turn, he has proved time and time again that is the Prime Minister of all Indians, going out of his way to make the Christian or the Muslim community aware that their welfare, he is as close to his heart, then the welfare of Hindus. Explain to your friends abroad that is primary focus has been to boost Indian economy and to foster good relationships with the neighbouring countries. You can also point out that the near hatred of the western media for him is totally irrational and not based on hard facts. As we said earlier for instance, the removal of articles 370 just set a wrong right – and any country would do that. Explain further that if England can claim the Falklands Islands, which rightfully belong to Argentina, ten thousand kilometres away from London, why cannot India retain Kashmir which has always been an integral part of its territory?

9. **Help India become the alternative to China**. Emphasize again and again on western national forums that *India is the natural economic and geopolitical partner of the West and the rest of the civilized world*. For contrary to China, it is democratic, pro-western, liberal, with a middle class as important as China's. Tell them that the Western powers have banked all their investments on China, neglecting India, the other giant of Asia, which is a grave mistake because some social upheaval is bound to happen in China sooner or later, as soon as the

authoritarian hold is removed one way or another. Highlight the fact that India is a much safer bet in the long run for western investments. Already India's PIB has overtaken the Chinese, who are facing a lot of economic difficulties. Tell them that at the very least, the US and Europe should balance their chips by investing half of them in India – the Prime Minister, Modi is in the process of liberalizing the economy and making it easier for foreign investors. Tell them that India is the next economic superpower and that it has a much better human rights record than China.

It is also very important that you point out that *India is the natural geopolitical buffer of the West in an Asia* racked by Islamic fundamentalism and the Chinese thirst for hegemony (explain to the British that Beijing is claiming for instance an Indian state as big as England – Arunachal Pradesh). Europe and the US also keep making the mistake of funding and arming Pakistan, even when they fully know that the Pakistanis have unleashed Islamic terrorism not only towards Kashmir, but unto the whole world.

10. Spread Happiness in the West. "India will become the spiritual leader of the world," Swami Vivekananda had predicted. Thus share with your Western friends the fact that hatha yoga, today practiced by hundreds of millions in the world, is a Hindu invention. Tell them too that Ayurveda, also taking the West by storm, is the oldest medical system still in practice in the world; that much before the West knew it used plants and minerals to cure people, knew that many illnesses have psychosomatic sources, and that Indian doctors practiced plastic surgery 1000 years before Christ. Talk about Pranayama, the most exacting, precise, mathematical, powerful breathing discipline one can dream of. Its effects and results have been observed and categorised by Indian yogis for millenniums. This extraordinary knowledge, brings in very quickly wonderful results in both the well being of the body and the quietude of the mind. Pushed to its extreme, it gives to the disciple deep spiritual experiences and a true inner perception of the world. Sri Sri Ravi Shankar has revitalized this science and packaged it in modern terms. Help them to practice meditation, queen of all the yogic sciences, that which is above everything, that without which any yogic discipline is impossible. That which interiorizes us, carries us within ourselves, to the discovery of our true soul and nature. There are hundreds of different mediation techniques, simple, cartesian, easy to experience, which have been devised by Indian sages since the dawn of Bharat. Each one has its own characteristics, each one gives particular results, which has been experienced by the billions of aspirants who have practised them since the dawn of Vedic times. This is the Wonder that IS Hinduism, tell them.

CHAPTER 40

The Idea of India Needs not be Recreated

Sri Aurobindo once said: everything is contained in the Vedas, the past present and the future. It is accepted today that Vedic spirituality and culture went **westwards** in ancient times: to Iran, where it created the religion of Zarathustra, to Greece, where many of the philosophies, gods and beliefs have a Vedic origin and even to Europe, where it influenced the Celtic culture. The Aryans went from India westwards and were not some white invaders, who imposed their might on the Dravidians and tribals.

The history of the invasions into India, particularly the Islamic ones, has never been told properly; In the words of American historian Will Durant: The *Islamic conquest* of India is probably the bloodiest story in history. It is a discouraging tale, for its evident moral is that civilization is a precious good, whose delicate complex of order and freedom, culture and peace, can at any moment be overthrown by barbarians *invading* from without or multiplying within ». These invasions have left deep scars in the psyche of Hindus today, of fear and terror.

The first prime minister of India, Jawaharlal Nehru, for good reason and bad reasons chose to bury under the carpet the history of these invasions. Maybe he thought that it was unnecessary to rake up the past when so many Muslims chose to remain in India. But no nation can move forward unless it looks squarely at its past. He also decided to borrow everything the British had left, educational, constitutional, judiciary, intellectual, without bothering to adapt it to the Indian psyche and the particular genius of India. this had disastrous consequences for India.

Indeed, The inheritance of Nehru is a heavy burden for India to bear, from the immerse bureaucracy, the corruption, the VVIP culture, which even the BJP is a victim of, the false idea of secularism which is an imposition of a western concept that has no bearing on an ancient culture that was universal and secular in nature: *vasudeva kutumbakam*, 'the whole World is my Family'. The idea that Hindutva is a dangerous element to secularism is thus preposterous.

It is true that there is an incredible diversity in India of cultures, religions, food, languages, customs, and that it makes for the beauty and attraction of this country. But we see that the assimilation phenomenon here has always been one way: no invader really managed to ever impose its own culture and religion on India, except but force, as Islam did, or by trickery and financial incentives, as Christian missionaries are still doing today.

But on the contrary they were influenced by the softening Hindu outlook, whether it is Indian Sufism, or some of the integrated Syrian Christians. But because of the growing impact of Sunni intolerance coming from Afghanistan, Pakistan and the Gulf countries, Islam in India has tended to go back to a certain rigidity, and Christianity as well because of protestant missionaries goes back to what my grandfather practiced. But these need not be permanent factors.

It is also true that there has been a degeneration of values in India and worldwide, what Hindus call **Kali Yuga**, the Age of Iron, corruption, environment degradation, westernization are today rampant in India. Thus, a new India, will have to overcome these flaws. Mr Modi, I think has started attempting all this.

Bu the idea of India need not be recreated, as it is already there in the words of Sri Aurobindo:

"India has the key to the knowledge and conscious application of the ideal of what she can do now, and with a new light, illumine; what was wrong and wry in her old methods she can now rectify; the fences which she

created to protect the outer growth of the spiritual ideal and which afterwards became barriers to its expansion and farther application, she can now break down and give her spirit a freer field and an ampler flight: she can, if she will, give a new and decisive turn to the problems over which all mankind is labouring and stumbling, for the clue to their solutions is there in her ancient knowledge."

Conclusion

While it is true that for many centuries, there were tremendous eras of Hindu power, whether Chandragupta, or Deva Raja of Vijaynagar.... While it is true also that Hindu power was always inclusive and accepted in its midst all kinds of religious, social and ethnic diversities.... While it is true, even more, that Hindu power was neither weak, nor absolutely and blindly nonviolent.... While it is true that it respected civilian lives and had certain rules of chivalry – will this kind of Hindu Power ever come back to India?

Though it is still true that Hindus today continue to incarnate this tolerance, acceptance and Supreme Knowledge of the mystery of Creation, understanding that the Divine maybe He or She, and takes different names at different times of our history, the conditions of this Planet have drastically changed. India has today many minorities that would not accept Hindu Power, however benevolent and soft it could be, Muslims, particularly, would not understand and tolerate a government that is wholly Hindu.

Many thought that Narendra Modi would again embody Hindu Power 450 years after the sack of Vijaynagar. But right from the beginning, in his first mandate, Modi took some distance from the Hindu cause, which he had fully embraced during his three terms as Chief Minister of Gujarat – and even while campaigning for the 2014 prime ministerial elections. Many hardcore Hindus were disappointed, but Narendra Modi, knowing the condition of the ground, probably took the right decision. He is the prime minister of a billion Indians, many of them Hindus of course, but with one hundred million Muslims, a sizable Christian population, Sikhs, Parsis, Jains, Jews, Armenians etc. Thus, it is probable that Hindu

Power, such as the one India knew in the past, may never come back to the subcontinent.

Nevertheless, the Hindu values that we all cherish: the smile on India's countrywomen whether they are from the North, the South, the East or the West, the tolerance, the capacity to integrate new values, while retaining ancient ones, the vast knowledge that Hinduism still carries – hatha yoga, ayurveda, pranayama, meditation, will survive, not only here in India, but also in the West, where they have taken root.

We will continue to love and worship this India that possesses Indu-ness, a quality that pervades every stratosphere of the country and that is imbedded in the genes of all Indians, particularly those in the rural areas. All of us, who live in this wonderful country that is called India, will be eternally grateful that this Hindu-ness has survived so many centuries of strife, travails, catastrophes, and obstacles. **This may be real Hindu Power.**